FEINHOCHBURG

Robert Lead's How To Be A Programmer

Robert Lead's How To Be A Programmer

ROBERT L. READ

FEINHOCHBURG
www.feinhochburg.com

Robert Read's How to be a Programmer

Published by

FEINHOCHBURG

www.feinhochburg.com

The original document can be found at

http://samizdat.mines.edu/howto/HowToBeAProgrammer.html

Printed in the USA

Dedication

To the programmers of Hire.com.

How To Be A Programmer

CONTENTS

Introduction

To be a good programmer is difficult and noble. The hardest part of making real a collective vision of a software project is dealing with one's coworkers and customers. Writing computer programs is important and takes great intelligence and skill. But it is really child's play compared to everything else that a good programmer must do to make a software system that succeeds for both the customer and myriad colleagues for whom she is partially responsible. In this essay I attempt to summarize as concisely as possible those things that I wish someone had explained to me when I was twenty-one.

This is very subjective and, therefore, this essay is doomed to be personal and somewhat opinionated. I confine myself to problems that a programmer is very likely to have to face in her work. Many of these problems and their solutions are so general to the human condition that I will probably seem preachy. I hope in spite of this that this essay will be useful.

Computer programming is taught in courses. The excellent books: The Pragmatic Programmer [Prag99], Code Complete [CodeC93], Rapid Development [RDev96], and Extreme Programming Explained [XP99] all teach computer programming and the larger issues of being a good programmer. The essays of Paul Graham[PGSite] and Eric Raymond[Hacker] should certainly be read before or along with this article. This essay differs from those excellent works by emphasizing social problems and comprehensively summarizing the entire set of necessary skills as I see them.

In this essay the term boss to refer to whomever gives you projects to do. I use the words business, company, and tribe, synonymously except that business connotes moneymaking, company connotes the modern workplace and tribe is generally the people you share loyalty with.

Welcome to the tribe.

How To Be A Programmer

Robert Read's
How To Be
A Programmer

Part 1
Beginner

Personal Skills

Learn to Debug

Debugging is the cornerstone of being a programmer. The first meaning of the verb to debug is to remove errors, but the meaning that really matters is to see into the execution of a program by examining it.

A programmer that cannot debug effectively is blind. Idealists that think design, or analysis, or complexity theory, or whatnot, are more fundamental are not working programmers. The working programmer does not live in an ideal world. Even if you are perfect, your are surrounded by and must interact with code written by major software companies, organizations like GNU, and your colleagues. Most of this code is imperfect and imperfectly documented. Without the ability to gain visibility into the execution of this code the slightest bump will throw you permanently. Often this visibility can only be gained by experimentation, that is, debugging.

Debugging is about the running of programs, not programs themselves. If you buy something from a major software company, you usually don't get to see the program. But there will still arise places where the code does not conform to the documentation (crashing your entire machine is a common and spectacular example), or where the documentation is mute. More commonly, you create an error, examine the code you wrote and have no clue how the error can be occurring. Inevitably, this means some assumption you are making is not quite correct, or some condition arises that you did not anticipate. Sometimes the magic trick of staring into the source code works. When it doesn't, you must debug.

To get visibility into the execution of a program you must be able to execute the code and observe something about it. Sometimes this is visible, like what is being displayed on a screen, or the delay between two events. In many other cases, it involves things that are not meant to be visible, like the state of some variables inside the code, which lines of code are actually being executed, or whether certain assertions hold across a complicated data structure. These hidden things must be revealed.

18

The common ways of looking into the 'innards' of an executing program can be categorized as:

- Using a debugging tool,

- Printlining — Making a temporary modification to the program, typically adding lines that print information out, and

- Logging — Creating a permanent window into the programs execution in the form of a log.

Debugging tools are wonderful when they are stable and available, but the printlining and logging are even more important. Debugging tools often lag behind language development, so at any point in time they may not be available. In addition, because the debugging tool may subtly change the way the program executes it may not always be practical. Finally, there are some kinds of debugging, such as checking an assertion against a large data structure, that require writing code and changing the execution of the program. It is good to know how to use debugging tools when they are stable, but it is critical to be able to employ the other two methods.

Some beginners fear debugging when it requires modifying code. This is understandable—it is a little like exploratory surgery. But you have to learn to poke at the code and make it jump; you have to learn to experiment on it, and understand that nothing that you temporarily do to it will make it worse. If you feel this fear, seek out a mentor—we lose a lot of good programmers at the delicate onset of their learning to this fear.

How to Debug by Splitting the Problem Space

Debugging is fun, because it begins with a mystery. You think it should do something, but instead it does something else. It is not always quite so simple—any examples I can give will be contrived compared to what sometimes happens in practice. Debugging requires creativity and ingenuity. If there is a single key to debugging is to use the divide and conquer technique on the mystery.

Suppose, for example, you created a program that should do ten things in a sequence. When you run it, it crashes. Since you didn't program it to crash, you now have a mystery. When out look at the output, you see that the first seven things in the sequence were run successfully. The last three are not visible from the output, so now your mystery is smaller: 'It crashed on thing #8, #9, or #10.'

Can you design an experiment to see which thing it crashed on? Sure. You can use a debugger or we can add printline statements (or the equivalent in whatever language you are working in) after #8 and #9. When we run it again, our mystery will be smaller, such as 'It crashed on thing #9.' I find that bearing in mind exactly what the mystery is at any point in time helps keep one focused. When several people are working together under pressure on a problem it is easy to forget what the most important mystery is.

The key to divide and conquer as a debugging technique is the same as it is for algorithm design: as long as you do a good job splitting the mystery in the middle, you won't have to split it too many times, and you will be debugging quickly. But what is the middle of a mystery? There is where true creativity and experience comes in.

To a true beginner, the space of all possible errors looks like every line in the source code. You don't have the vision you will later develop to see the other dimensions of the program, such as the space of executed lines, the data structure, the memory management, the interaction with foreign code, the code that is risky, and the code that is simple. For the experience programmer, these other dimensions form an imperfect but very useful mental model of all the things that can go wrong. Having that mental model is what helps one find the middle of the mystery effectively.

Once you have evenly subdivided the space of all that can go wrong, you must try to decide in which space the error lies. In the simple case where the mystery is: 'Which single unknown line makes my program crash?', you can ask yourself: 'Is the unknown line executed before or after this line that I judge to be executed in the about the middle of the running program?' Usually you will not be so lucky as to know that the error exists in a single line, or even a single block. Often the mystery will be more like: 'Either there is a pointer in that graph that points to the wrong node, or my algorithm that adds up the variables in that graph doesn't work.' In that case you may have to write a small program to check that the pointers in the graph are all correct in order to decide which part of the subdivided mystery can be eliminated.

How to Remove an Error

I've intentionally separated the act of examining a program's execution from the act of fixing an error. But of course, *debugging* does also mean removing the bug. Ideally you will have perfect understanding of the code and will reach an 'A-Ha!' moment where you perfectly see the error and how to fix it. But since your program will often use insufficiently documented systems into which you have no visibility, this is not always possible. In other cases the code is so complicated that your understanding cannot be perfect.

In fixing a bug, you want to make the smallest change that fixes the bug. You may see other things that need improvement; but don't fix those at the same time. Attempt to employ the scientific method of changing one thing and only one thing at a time. The best process for this is to be able to easily reproduce the bug, then put your fix in place, and then rerun the program and observe that the bug no longer exists. Of course, sometimes more than one line must be changed, but you should still conceptually apply a single atomic change to fix the bug.

Sometimes, there are really several bugs that look like one. It is up to you to define the bugs and fix them one at a time. Sometimes it is unclear what the program should do or what the original author intended. In this case, you must exercise your experience and judgment and assign your own meaning to the code. Decide what it should do, and comment it or clarify it in some way and then make the code conform to your meaning. This is an intermediate or advanced skill that is sometimes harder than writing the original function in the first place, but the real world is often messy. You may have to fix a system you cannot rewrite.

How to Debug Using a Log

Logging is the practice of writing a system so that it produces a sequence of informative records, called a log. Printlining is just producing a simple, usually temporary, log. Absolute beginners must understand and use logs because their knowledge of the programming is limited; system architects must understand and use logs because of the complexity of the system. The amount of information that is provided by the log should be configurable, ideally while the program is running. In general, logs offer three basic advantages:

- Logs can provide useful information about bugs that are hard to reproduce (such as those that occur in the production environment but that cannot be reproduced in the test environment).

- Logs can provide statistics and data relevant to performance, such as the time passing between statements.

- When configurable, logs allow general information to be captured in order to debug unanticipated specific problems without having to modify and/or redeploy the code just to deal with those specific problems.

The amount to output into the log is always a compromise between information and brevity. Too much information makes the log expensive and produces scroll blindness, making it hard to find the information you need. Too little information and it may not contain what you need. For this reason, making what is output configurable is very useful. Typically, each record in the log will identify its position in the source code, the thread that executed it if applicable, the precise time of execution, and, commonly, an additional useful piece of information, such as the value of some variable, the amount of free memory, the number of data objects, etc. These log statements are sprinkled throughout the source code but are particularly at major functionality points and around risky code. Each statement can be assigned a level and will only output a record if the system is currently configured to output that level. You should design the log statements to address problems that you anticipate. Anticipate the need to measure performance.

If you have a permanent log, printlining can now be done in terms of the log records, and some of the debugging statements will probably be permanently added to the logging system.

How to Understand Performance Problems

Learning to understand the performance of a running system is unavoidable for the same reason that learning debugging is. Even if the code you understand perfectly precisely the cost of the code you write, your code will make calls into other software systems that you have little control over or visibility into. However, in practice performance problems are a little different and a little easier than debugging in general.

Suppose that you or your customers consider a system or a subsystem to be too slow. Before you try to make it faster, you must build a mental model of why it is slow. To do this you can use a profiling tool or a good log to figure out where the time or other resources are really being spent. There is a famous dictum that 90% of the time will be spent in 10% of the code. I would add to that the importance of input/output expense (I/O) to performance issues. Often most of the time is spent in I/O in one way or another. Finding the expensive I/O and the expensive 10% of the code is a good first step to building your mental model.

There are many dimensions to the performance of a computer system, and many resources consumed. The first resource to measure is wall-clock time, the total time that passes for the computation. Logging wall-clock time is particularly valuable because it can inform about unpredictable circumstance that arise in situations where other profiling is impractical. However, this may not always represent the whole picture. Sometimes something that takes a little longer but doesn't burn up so many processor seconds will be much better in computing environment you actually have to deal with. Similarly, memory, network bandwidth, database or other server accesses may, in the end, be far more expensive than processor seconds.

Contention for shared resources that are synchronized can cause deadlock and starvation. Deadlock is the inability to proceed because of improper synchronization or resource demands. Starvation is the failure to schedule a component properly. If it can be at all anticipated, it is best to have a way of measuring this contention from the start of your project. Even if this contention does not occur, it is very helpful to be able to assert that with confidence.

How to Fix Performance Problems

Most software projects can be made with relatively little effort 10 to 100 times faster than they are at the they are first released. Under time-to-market pressure, it is both wise and effective to choose a solution that gets the job done simply and quickly, but less efficiently than some other solution. However, performance is a part of usability, and often it must eventually be considered more carefully.

The key to improving the performance of a very complicated system is to analyze it well enough to find the bottlenecks, or places where most of the resources are consumed. There is not much sense in optimizing a function that accounts for only 1% of the computation time. As a rule of thumb you should think carefully before doing anything unless you think it is going to make the system or a significant part of it at least twice as fast. There is usually a way to do this. Consider the test and quality assurance effort that your change will require. Each change brings a test burden with it, so it is much better to have a few big changes.

After you've made a two-fold improvement in something, you need to at least rethink and perhaps reanalyze to discover the next-most-expensive bottleneck in the system, and attack that to get another two-fold improvement.

Often, the bottlenecks in performance will be an example of counting cows by counting legs and dividing by four, instead of counting heads. For example, I've made errors such as failing to provide a relational database system with a proper index on a column I look up a lot, which probably made it at least 20 times slower. Other examples include doing unnecessary I/O in inner loops, leaving in debugging statements that are no longer needed, unnecessary memory allocation, and, in particular, inexpert use of libraries and other subsystems that are often poorly documented with respect to performance. This kind of improvement is sometimes called low-hanging fruit, meaning that it can be easily picked to provide some benefit.

What do you do when you start to run out of low-hanging fruit? Well, you can reach higher, or chop the tree down. You can continue making small improvements or you can seriously redesign a system or a subsystem. (This is a great opportunity to use your skills as a good programmer, not only in the new design but also in convincing your boss that this is a good idea.) However, before you argue for the redesign of a subsystem, you should ask yourself whether or not your proposal will make it five to ten time better.

How to Optimize Loops

Sometimes you'll encounter loops, or recursive functions, that take a long time to execute and are bottlenecks in your product. Before you try to make the loop a little faster, but spend a few minutes considering if there is a way to remove it entirely. Would a different algorithm do? Could you compute that while computing something else? If you can't find away around it, then you can optimize the loop. This is simple; move stuff out. In the end, this will require not only ingenuity but also an understanding of the expense of each kind of statement and expression.

Here are some suggestions:

- Remove floating point operations.
- Don't allocate new memory blocks unnecessarily.
- Fold constants together.
- Move I/O into a buffer.
- Try not to divide.
- Try not to do expensive typecasts.
- Move a pointer rather than recomputing indices.

The cost of each of these operations depends on your specific system. On some systems compilers and hardware do these things for you. Clear, efficient code is better than code that requires an understanding of a particular platform.

How to Deal with I/O Expense

For a lot of problems, processors are fast compared to the cost of communicating with a hardware device. This cost is usually abbreviated I/O, and can include network cost, disk I/O, database queries, file I/O, and other use of some hardware not very close to the processor. Therefore building a fast system is often more a question of improving I/O than improving the code in some tight loop, or even improving an algorithm.

There are two very fundamental techniques to improving I/O: caching and representation. Caching is avoiding I/O (generally avoiding the reading of some abstract value) by storing a copy of that value locally so no I/O is performed to get the value. The first key to caching is to make it crystal clear which data is the master and which are copies. There is only one master—period. Caching brings with it the danger that the copy is sometimes can't reflect changes to the master instantaneously.

Representation is the approach of making I/O cheaper by representing data more efficiently. This is often in tension with other demands, like human readability and portability.

Representations can often be improved by a factor of two or three from their first implementation. Techniques for doing this include using a binary representation instead of one that is human readable, transmitting a dictionary of symbols along with the data so that long symbols don't have to be encoded, and, at the extreme, things like Huffman encoding.

A third technique that is sometimes possible is to improve the locality of reference by pushing the computation closer to the data. For instance, if you are reading some data from a database and computing something simple from it, such as a summation, try to get the database server to do it for you. This is highly dependent on the kind of system you're working with, but you should explore it.

How to Manage Memory

Memory is a precious resource that you can't afford to run out of. You can ignore it for a while but eventually you will have to decide how to manage memory.

Space that needs to persist beyond the scope of a single subroutine is often called heap allocated. A chunk of memory is useless, hence garbage, when nothing refers to it. Depending on the system you use, you may have to explicitly deallocate memory yourself when it is about to become garbage. More often you may be able to use a system that provides a garbage collector. A garbage collector notices garbage and frees its space without any action required by the programmer. Garbage collection is wonderful: it lessens errors and increases code brevity and concision cheaply. Use it when you can.

But even with garbage collection, you can fill up all memory with garbage. A classic mistake is to use a hash table as a cache and forget to remove the references in the hash table. Since the reference remains, the referent is noncollectable but useless. This is called a memory leak. You should look for and fix memory leaks early. If you have long running systems memory may never be exhausted in testing but will be exhausted by the user.

The creation of new objects is moderately expensive on any system. Memory allocated directly in the local variables of a subroutine, however, is usually cheap because the policy for freeing it can be very simple. You should avoid unnecessary object creation.

An important case occurs when you can define an upper bound on the number of objects you will need at one time. If these objects all take up the same amount of memory, you may be able to allocate a single block of memory, or a buffer, to hold them all. The objects you need can be allocated and released inside this buffer in a set rotation pattern, so it is sometimes called a ring buffer. This is usually faster than heap allocation.

Sometimes you have to explicitly free allocated space so it can be reallocated rather than rely on garbage collection. Then you must apply careful intelligence to each chunk of allocated memory and design a way for it to be deallocated at the appropriate time. The method may differ for each kind of object you create. You must make sure that every execution of a memory allocating operation is matched by a memory deallocating operation eventually. This is so difficult that programmers often simply implement a rudimentary form or garbage collection, such as reference counting, to do this for them.

How to Deal with Intermittent Bugs

The intermittent bug is a cousin of the 50-foot-invisible-scorpion-from-outer-space kind of bug. This nightmare occurs so rarely that it is hard to observe, yet often enough that it can't be ignored. You can't debug because you can't find it.

Although after 8 hours you will start to doubt it, the intermittent bug has to obey the same laws of logic everything else does. What makes it hard is that it occurs only under unknown conditions. Try to record the circumstances under which the bug does occur, so that you can guess at what the variability really is. The condition may be related to data values, such as 'This only happens when we enter *Wyoming* as a value.' If that is not the source of variability, the next suspect should be improperly synchronized concurrency.

Try, try, try to reproduce the bug in a controlled way. If you can't reproduce it, set a trap for it by building a logging system, a special one if you have to, that can log what you guess you need when it really does occur. Resign yourself to that if the bug only occurs in production and not at your whim, this is may be a long process. The hints that you get from the log may not provide the solution but may give you enough information to improve the logging. The improved logging system may take a long time to be put into production. Then, you have to wait for the bug to reoccur to get more information. This cycle can go on for some time.

The stupidest intermittent bug I ever created was in a multi-threaded implementation of a functional programming language for a class project. I had very carefully insured correct concurrent evaluation of the functional program, good utilization of all the CPUs available (eight, in this case). I simply forgot to synchronize the garbage collector. The system could run a long time, often finishing whatever task I began, before anything noticeable went wrong. I'm ashamed to admit I had begun to question the hardware before my mistake dawned on me.

At work we recently had an intermittent bug that took us several weeks to find. We have multi-threaded application servers in Java™ behind Apache™ web servers. To maintain fast page turns, we do all I/O in small set of four separate threads that are different than the page-turning threads. Every once in a while these would apparently get 'stuck' and cease doing anything useful, so far as our logging allowed us to tell, for hours. Since we had four threads, this was not in itself a giant problem --- unless all four got stuck. Then the queues emptied by these threads would quickly fill up all available memory and crash our server. It took us about a week to figure this much out, and we still didn't know what caused it, when it would happen, or even what the threads where doing when they got 'stuck'.

This illustrates some risk associated with third-party software. We were using a licensed piece of code that removed HTML tags from text. Due to its place of origin we affectionately referred to this as 'the French stripper.' Although we had the source code (thank goodness!) we had not studied it carefully until by turning up the logging on our servers we finally realized that the email threads were getting stuck in the French stripper.

The stripper performed well except on some long and unusual kinds of texts. On these texts, the code was quadratic or worse. This means that the processing time was proportional to the square of the length of the text. Had these texts occurred commonly, we would have found the bug right away. If they had never occurred at all, we would never have had a problem. As it happens, it took us weeks to finally understand and resolve the problem.

How to Learn Design Skills

To learn how to design software, study the action of a mentor by being physically present when they are designing. Then study well-written pieces of software. After that, you can read some books on the latest design techniques.

Then you must do it yourself. Start with a small project. When you are finally done, consider how the design failed or succeeded and how you diverged from your original conception. They move on to larger projects, hopefully in conjunction with other people. Design is a matter of judgment that takes years to acquire. A smart programmer can learn the basics adequately in two months and can improve from there.

It is natural and helpful to develop your own style, but remember that design is an art, not a science. People who write books on the subject have a vested interest in making it seem scientific. Don't become dogmatic about particular design styles.

How to Conduct Experiments

The late, great Edsger Dijkstra has eloquently explained that Computer Science is not an experimental science[ExpCS] and doesn't depend on electronic computers. As he puts it referring to the 1960s[Knife],

> *...the harm was done: the topic became known as "computer science"—which, actually, is like referring to surgery as "knife science" — and it was firmly implanted in people's minds that computing science is about machines and their peripheral equipment.*

Programming ought not to be an experimental science, but most working programmers do not have the luxury of engaging in what Dijkstra means by computing science. We must work in the realm of experimentation, just as some, but not all, physicists do. If thirty years from now programming can be performed without experimentation, it will be a great accomplishment of Computer Science.

The kinds of experiments you will have to perform include:
- Testing systems with small examples to verify that they conform to the documentation or to understand their response when there is no documentation,
- Testing small code changes to see if they actually fix a bug,
- Measuring the performance of a system under two different conditions due to imperfect knowledge of there performance characteristics,
- Checking the integrity of data, and
- Collecting statistics that may hint at the solution to difficult or hard-to-repeat bugs.

I don't think in this essay I can explain the design of experiments; you will have to study and practice. However, I can offer two bits of advice. First, try to be very clear about your hypothesis, or the assertion that you are trying to test. It also helps to write the hypothesis down, especially if you find yourself confused or are working with others.

You will often find yourself having to design a series of experiments, each of which is based on the knowledge gained from the last experiment. Therefore, you should design your experiments to provide the most information possible. Unfortunately, this is in tension with keeping each experiment simple --- you will have to develop this judgment through experience.

Team Skills

Why Estimation is Important

To get a working software system in active use as quickly as possible requires not only planning the development, but also planning the documentation, deployment, marketing. In a commercial project it also requires sales and finance. Without predictability of the development time, it is impossible to plan these effectively.

Good estimation provides predictability. Managers love it, as well they should. The fact that it is impossible, both theoretically and practically, to predict accurately how long it will take to develop software is often lost on managers. We are asked to do this impossible thing all the time, and we must face up to it honestly. However, it would be dishonest not to admit the impossibility of this task, and when necessary, explain it. There is a lot of room for miscommunication about estimates, as people have a startling tendency to think wishfully that the sentence:

> *I estimate that, if I really understand the problem, it is about 50% likely that we will be done in five weeks (if no one bothers us during that time).*

really means:

> *I promise to have it all done five weeks from now.*

This common interpretation problem requires that you explicitly discuss what the estimate means with your boss or customer as if they were a simpleton. Restate your assumptions, no matter how obvious they seem to you.

31

How to Estimate Programming Time

Estimation takes practice. It also takes labor. It takes so much labor it may be a good idea to estimate the time it will take to make the estimate, especially if you are asked to estimate something big.

When asked to provide an estimate of something big, the most honest thing to do is to stall. Most engineers are enthusiastic and eager to please, and stalling certainly will displease the stalled. But an on-the-spot estimate probably won't be accurate and honest.

While stalling, it may be possible to consider doing or prototyping the task. If political pressure permits, this is the most accurate way of producing the estimate, and it makes real progress.

When not possible to take the time for some investigation, you should first establish the meaning of the estimate very clearly. Restate that meaning as the first and last part of your written estimate. Prepare a written estimate by deconstructing the task into progressively smaller subtasks until each small task is no more than a day; ideally at most in length. The most important thing is not to leave anything out. For instance, documentation, testing, time for planning, time for communicating with other groups, and vacation time are all very important. If you spend part of each day dealing with knuckleheads, put a line item for that in the estimate. This gives your boss visibility into what is using up your time at a minimum, and might get you more time.

I know good engineers who pad estimates implicitly, but I recommend that you do not. One of the results of padding is trust in you may be depleted. For instance, an engineer might estimate three days for a task that she truly thinks will take one day. The engineer may plan to spend two days documenting it, or two days working on some other useful project. But it will be detectable that the task was done in only one day (if it turns out that way), and the appearance of slacking or overestimating is born. It's far better to give proper visibility into what you are actually doing. If documentation takes twice as long as coding and the estimate says so, tremendous advantage is gained by making this visible to the manager.

Pad explicitly instead. If a task will probably take one day—but might take ten days if your approach doesn't work—note this somehow in the estimate if you can; if not, at least do an average weighted by your estimates of the probabilities. Any risk factor that you can identify and assign an estimate to should go into the schedule. One person is unlikely to be sick in any given week. But a large project with many engineers will have some sick time; likewise vacation time. And what is the probability of a mandatory company-wide training seminar? If it can be estimated, stick it in. There are of course, unknown unknowns, or unk-unks. Unk-unks by definition cannot be estimated individually. You can try to create a global line item for all unk-unks, or handle them in some other way that you communicate to your boss. You cannot, however, let your boss forget that they exist, and it is devilishly easy for an estimate to become a schedule without the unk-unks considered.

In a team environment, you should try to have the people who will do the work do the estimate, and you should try to have team-wide consensus on estimates. People vary widely in skill, experience, preparedness, and confidence. Calamity strikes when a strong programmer estimates for herself and then weak programmers are held to this estimate. The act of having the whole team agree on a line-by-line basis to the estimate clarifies the team understanding, as well as allowing the opportunity for tactical reassignment of resources (for instance, shifting burden away from weaker team members to stronger).

If there are big risks that cannot be evaluated, it is your duty to state so forcefully enough that your manager does not commit to them and then become embarrassed when the risk occurs. Hopefully in such a case whatever is needed will be done to decrease the risk.

If you can convince your company to use Extreme Programming, you will only have to estimate relatively small things, and this is both more fun and more productive.

How to Find Out Information

The nature of what you need to know determines how you should find it.

33

If you need information *about concrete things* that are objective and easy to verify, for example the latest patch level of a software product, ask a large number of people politely by searching the internet for it or by posting on a discussion group. Don't search on the internet for anything that smacks of either opinion or subjective interpretation: the ratio of drivel to truth is too high.

If you need *general knowledge about something subjective* the history of what people have thought about it, go to the library (the physical building in which books are stored). For example, to learn about math or mushrooms or mysticism, go to the library.

If you need to know *how to do something that is not trivial* get two or three books on the subject and read them. You might learn how to do something trivial, like install a software package, from the Internet. You can even learn important things, like good programming technique, but you can easily spend more time searching and sorting the results and attempting to divine the authority of the results than it would take to read the pertinent part of a solid book.

If you need *information that no one else could be expected to know* for example, 'does this software that is brand new work on gigantic data sets?', you must still search the internet and the library. After those options are completely exhausted, you may design an experiment to ascertain it.

If you want an opinion or a value judgment that takes into account some unique circumstance, talk to an expert. For instance, if you want to know whether or not it is a good idea to build a modern database management system in LISP, you should talk to a LISP expert and a database expert.

If you want to know *how likely it is* that a faster algorithm for a particular application exists that has not yet been published, talk to someone working in that field.

If you want to make a *personal decision that only you can make* like whether or not you should start a business, try putting into writing a list of arguments for and against the idea. If that fails, consider divination.

Suppose you have studied the idea from all angles, have done all your homework, and worked out all the consequences and pros and cons in your mind, and yet still remain indecisive. You now must follow your heart and tell your brain to shut up. The multitude of available divination techniques are very useful for determining your own semi-conscious desires, as they each present a complete ambiguous and random pattern that your own subconscious will assign meaning to.

How to Utilize People as Information Sources

Respect every person's time and balance it against your own. Asking someone a question accomplishes far more than just receiving the answer. The person learns about you, both by enjoying your presence and hearing the particular question. You learn about the person in the same way, and you may learn the answer you seek. This is usually far more important than your question.

However, the value of this diminishes the more you do it. You are, after all, using the most precious commodity a person has: their time. The benefits of communication must be weighed against the costs. Furthermore, the particular costs and benefits derived differ from person to person. I strongly believe that an executive of 100 people should spend five minutes a month talking to each person in her organization, which would be about 5% of their time. But ten minutes might be too much, and five minutes is too much if they have one thousand employees. The amount of time you spend talking to each person in your organization depends on their role (more than their position). You should talk to your boss more than your boss's boss, but you should talk to your boss's boss a little. It may be uncomfortable, but I believe you have a duty to talk a little bit to all your superiors, each month, no matter what.

The basic rule is that everyone benefits from talking to you a little bit, and the more they talk to you, the less benefit they derive. It is your job to provide them this benefit, and to get the benefit of communicating with them, keeping the benefit in balance with the time spent.

It is important to respect your own time. If talking to someone, even if it will cost them time, will save you a great deal of time, then you should do it unless you think their time is more valuable than yours, to the tribe, by that factor.

35

A strange example of this is the summer intern. A summer intern in a highly technical position can't be expected to accomplish too much; they can be expected to pester the hell out of everybody there. So why is this tolerated? Because the pestered are receiving something important from the intern. They get a chance to showoff a little. They get a chance to hear some new ideas, maybe; they get a chance to see things from a different perspective. They may also be trying to recruit the intern, but even if this is not the case there is much to gain.

You should ask people for a little bit of their wisdom and judgment whenever you honestly believe they have something to say. This flatters them and you will learn something and teach them something. A good programmer does not often need the advice of a Vice President of Sales, but if you ever do, you be sure to ask for it. I once asked to listen in on a few sales calls to better understand the job of our sales staff. This took no more than 30 minutes but I think that small effort made an impression on the sales force.

How to Document Wisely

Life is too short to write crap nobody will read; if you write crap, nobody will read it. Therefore a little good documentation is best. Managers often don't understand this, because even bad documentation gives them a false sense of security that they are not dependent on their programmers. If someone absolutely insists that you write truly useless documentation, say „yes" and quietly begin looking for a better job.

There's nothing quite as effective as putting an accurate estimate of the amount of time it will take to produce good documentation into an estimate to slacken the demand for documentation. The truth is cold and hard: documentation, like testing, can take many times longer than developing code.

Writing good documentation is, first of all, good writing. I suggest you find books on writing, study them, and practice. But even if you are a lousy writer or have poor command of the language in which you must document, the Golden Rule is all you really need: „Do unto others as you would have them do unto you." Take time to really think about who will be reading your documentation, what they need to get out of it, and how you can teach that to them. If you do that, you will be an above average documentation writer, and a good programmer.

When it comes to actually documenting code itself, as opposed to producing documents that can actually be read by non-programmers, the best programmers I've ever known hold a universal sentiment: write self-explanatory code and only document code in the places that you cannot make it clear by writing the code itself. There are two good reasons for this. First, anyone who needs to see code-level documentation will in most cases be able to and prefer to read the code anyway. Admittedly, this seems easier to the experienced programmer than to the beginner. More importantly however, is that the code and the documentation cannot be inconsistent if there is no documentation. The source code can at worst be wrong and confusing. The documentation, if not written perfectly, can lie, and that is a thousand times worse.

This does not make it easier on the responsible programmer. How does one write self-explanatory code? What does that even mean? It means:

- Writing code knowing that someone will have to read it;

- Applying the golden rule;

- Choosing a solution that is straightforward, even if you could get by with another solution faster;

- Sacrificing small optimizations that obfuscate the code;

- Thinking about the reader and spending some of your precious time to make it easier on her; and

- Not ever using a function name like „foo",„bar", or „doIt"!

How to Work with Poor Code

It is very common to have to work with poor quality code that someone else has written. Don't think too poorly of them, however, until you have walked in their shoes. They may have been asked very consciously to get something done quickly to meet schedule pressure. Regardless, in order to work with unclear code you must understand it. To understand it takes learning time, and that time will have to come out of some schedule, somewhere, and you must insist on it. To understand it, you will have to read the source code. You will probably have to experiment with it.

This is a good time to document, even if it is only for yourself, because the act of trying to document the code will force you to consider angles you might not have considered, and the resulting document may be useful. While you're doing this, consider what it would take to rewrite some or all of the code. Would it actually save time to rewrite some of it? Could you trust it better if you rewrote it? Be careful of arrogance here. If you rewrite it, it will be easier for you to deal with, but will it really be easier for the next person who has to read it? If you rewrite it, what will the test burden be? Will the need to re-test it outweigh any benefits that might be gained?

In any estimate that you make for work against code you didn't write, the quality of that code should affect your perception of the risk of problems and unk-unks.

It is important to remember that abstraction and encapsulation, two of a programmer's best tools, are particularly applicable to lousy code. You may not be able to redesign a large block of code, but if you can add a certain amount of abstraction to it you can obtain some of the benefits of a good design without reworking the whole mess. In particular, you can try to wall off the parts that are particularly bad so that they may be redesigned independently.

How to Use Source Code Control

Source code control systems let you manage projects effectively. They're very useful for one person and essential for a group. They track all changes in different versions so that no code is ever lost and meaning can be assigned to changes. One can create throw-away and debugging code with confidence with a source code control system, since the code you modify is kept carefully separate from committed, official code that will be shared with the team or released.

I was late to appreciate the benefits of source code control systems but now I wouldn't live without one even on a one-person project. Generally they are necessary when you have team working on the same code base. However, they have another great advantage: they encourage thinking about the code as a growing, organic system. Since each change is marked as a new revision with a new name or number, one begins to think of the software as a visibly progressive series of improvements. I think this is especially useful for beginners.

A good technique for using a source code control system is to stay within a few days of being up-to-date at all time. Code that can't be finished in a few days is checked in, but in a way that it is inactive and will not be called, and therefore not create any problems for anybody else. Committing a mistake that slows down your teammates is a serious error; it is often taboo.

How to Unit Test

Unit testing, the testing of an individual piece of coded functionality by the team that wrote it, is a part of coding, not something different from it. Part of designing the code is designing how it will be tested. You should write down a test plan, even if it is only one sentence. Sometimes the test will be simple: „Does the button look good?" Sometimes it will be complex: „Did this matching algorithm return precisely the correct matches?"

Use assertion checking and test drivers whenever possible. This not only catches bugs early, but is very useful later on and lets you eliminate mysteries that you would otherwise have to worry about.

The Extreme Programming developers are writing extensively on unit testing effectively; I can do no better than to recommend their writings.

Take Breaks when Stumped

When stumped, take a break. I sometimes meditate for 15 minutes when stumped and the problem magically unravels when I come back to it. A night's sleep sometimes does the same thing on a larger scale. It's possible that temporarily switching to any other activity may work.

How to Recognize When to Go Home

Computer programming is an activity that is also a culture. The unfortunate fact is that it is not a culture that values mental or physical health very much. For both cultural/historical reasons (the need to work at night on unloaded computers, for example) and because of overwhelming time-to-market pressure and the scarcity of programmers, computer programmers are traditionally overworked. I don't think you can trust all the stories you hear, but I think 60 hours a week is common, and 50 is pretty much a minimum. This means that often much more than that is required. This is serious problem for a good programmer, who is responsible not only for themselves but their teammates as well. You have to recognize when to go home, and sometimes when to suggest that other people go home. There can't be any fixed rules for solving this problem, anymore than there can be fixed rules for raising a child, for the same reason --- every human being is different.

Beyond 60 hours a week is an extraordinary effort for me, which I can apply for short periods of time (about one week), and that is sometimes expected of me. I don't know if it is fair to expect 60 hours of work from a person; I don't even know if 40 is fair. I am sure, however, that it is stupid to work so much that you are getting little out of that extra hour you work. For me personally, that's any more than 60 hours a week. I personally think a programmer should exercise noblesse oblige and shoulder a heavy burden. However, it is not a programmer's duty to be a patsy. The sad fact is programmers *are* often asked to be patsies in order to put on a show for somebody, for example a manager trying to impress an executive. Programmers often succumb to this because they are eager to please and not very good at saying no.

There are four defenses against this:

- Communicate as much as possible with everyone in the company so that no one can mislead the executives about what is going on,

- Learn to estimate and schedule defensively and explicitly and give everyone visibility into what the schedule is and where it stands,

- Learn to say no, and say no as a team when necessary, and

- Quit if you have to.

Most programmers are good programmers, and good programmers want to get a lot done. To do that, they have to manage their time effectively. There is a certain amount of mental inertia associated with getting warmed-up to a problem and deeply involved in it. Many programmers find they work best when they have long, uninterrupted blocks of time in which to get warmed-up and concentrate. However, people must sleep and perform other duties. Each person needs to find a way to satisfy both their human rhythm and their work rhythm. Each programmer needs to do whatever it takes to procure efficient work periods, such as reserving certain days in which you will attend only the most critical meetings.

Since I have children, I try to spend evenings with them sometimes. The rhythm that works best for me is to work a very long day, sleep in the office or near the office (I have a long commute from home to work) then go home early enough the next day to spend time with my children before they go to bed. I am not comfortable with this, but it is the best compromise I have been able to work out. Go home if you have a contagious disease. You should go home if you are thinking suicidal thoughts. You should take a break or go home if you think homicidal thoughts for more than a few seconds. You should send someone home if they show serious mental malfunctioning or signs of mental illness beyond mild depression. If you are tempted to be dishonest or deceptive in a way that you normally are not due to fatigue, you should take a break. Don't use cocaine or amphetamines to combat fatigue. Don't abuse caffeine.

How to Deal with Difficult People

You will probably have to deal with difficult people. You may even be a difficult person yourself. If you are the kind of person who has a lot of conflicts with coworkers and authority figures, you should cherish the independence this implies, but work on your interpersonal skills without sacrificing your intelligence or principles.

This can be very disturbing to some programmers who have no experience in this sort of thing and whose previous life experience has taught them patterns of behavior that are not useful in the workplace. Difficult people are often inured to disagreement and they are less affected by social pressure to compromise than others. The key is to respect them appropriately, which is more than you will want to but not as much as they might want.

Programmers have to work together as a team. When disagreement arises, it must be resolved somehow, it cannot be ducked for long. Difficult people are often extremely intelligent and have something very useful to say. It is critical that you listen and understand the difficult person without prejudice caused by the person. A failure to communicate is often the basis of disagreement but it can sometimes be removed with great patience. Try to keep this communication cool and cordial, and don't accept any baits for greater conflict that may be offered. After a reasonable period of trying to understand, make a decision.

Don't let a bully force you to do something you don't agree with. If you are the leader, do what you think is best. Don't make a decision for any personal reasons, and be prepared to explain the reasons for your decision. If you are a teammate with a difficult person, don't let the leader's decision have any personal impact. If it doesn't go your way, do it the other way whole-heartedly.

Difficult people do change and improve. I've seen it with my own eyes, but it is very rare. However, everyone has transitory ups and downs.

One of the challenges that every programmer but especially leaders face is keeping the difficult person fully engaged. They are more prone to duck work and resist passively than others.

42

Part 2
Intermediate

Personal Skills

How to Stay Motivated

It is a wonderful and surprising fact that programmers are highly motivated by the desire to create artifacts that are beautiful, useful, or nifty. This desire is not unique to programmers nor universal but it is so strong and common among programmers that it separates them from others in other roles.

This has practical and important consequences. If programmers are asked to do something that is not beautiful, useful, or nifty, they will have low morale. There's a lot of money to be made doing ugly, stupid, and boring stuff; but in the end, fun will make the most money for the company.

Obviously, there are entire industries organized around motivational techniques some of which apply here. The things that are specific to programming that I can identify are:
- Use the best language for the job.
- Look for opportunities to apply new techniques, languages, and technologies.
- Try to either learn or teach something, however small, in each project.

Finally, if possible, measure the impact of your work in terms of something that will be personally motivating. For example, when fixing bugs, counting the number of bugs that I have fixed is not at all motivational to me, because it is independent of the number that may still exist, and is also affects the total value I'm adding to my company's customers in only the smallest possible way. Relating each bug to a happy customer, however, *is* personally motivating to me.

How to be Widely Trusted

To be trusted you must be trustworthy. You must also be visible. If no one knows about you, no trust will be invested in you. With those close to you, such as your teammates, this should not be an issue. You establish trust by being responsive and informative to those outside your department or team. Occasionally someone will abuse this trust, and ask for unreasonable favors. Don't be afraid of this, just explain what you would have to give up doing to perform the favor.

Don't pretend to know something that you don't. With people that are not teammates, you may have to make a clear distinction between „not knowing right off the top of my head" and „not being able to figure it out, ever."

How to Tradeoff Time vs. Space

You can be a good programmer without going to college, but you can't be a good intermediate programmer without knowing basic computational complexity theory. You don't need to know „big O" notation, but I personally think you should be able to understand the difference between „constant-time",„n log n" and „n squared". You might be able to intuit how to tradeoff time against space without this knowledge, but in its absence you will not have a firm basis for communicating with your colleagues.

In designing or understanding an algorithm, the amount of time it takes to run is sometimes a function of the size of the input. When that is true, we can say an algorithm's worst/expected/best-case running time is „n log n" if it is proportional to the size (n) times the logarithm of the size. The notation and way of speaking can be also be applied to the space taken up by a data structure.

To me, computational complexity theory is beautiful and as profound as physics—and a little bit goes a long way!

Time (processor cycles) and space (memory) can be traded off against each other. Engineering is about compromise, and this is a fine example. It is not always systematic. In general, however, one can save space by encoding things more tightly, at the expense of more computation time when you have to decode them. You can save time by caching, that is, spending space to store a local copy of something, at the expense of having to maintain the consistency of the cache. You can sometimes save time by maintaining more information in a data structure. This usually cost a small amount of space but may complicate the algorithm.

Improving the space/time tradeoff can often change one or the other dramatically. However, before you work on this you should ask yourself if what you are improving is really the thing that needs the most improvement. It's fun to work on an algorithm, but you can't let that blind you to the cold hard fact that improving something that is not a problem will not make any noticeable difference and will create a test burden.

Memory on modern computers appears cheap, because unlike processor time, you can't see it being used until you hit the wall; but then failure is catastrophic. There are also other hidden costs to using memory, such as your effect on other programs that must be resident, and the time to allocate and deallocate it. Consider this carefully before you trade away space to gain speed.

How to Stress Test

Stress testing is fun. At first it appears that the purpose of stress testing is to find out if the system works under a load. In reality, it is common that the system does work under a load but fails to work in some way when the load is heavy enough. I call this *hitting the wall* or *bonking*[1]. There may be some exceptions, but there is almost always a 'wall'. The purpose of stress testing is to figure out where the wall is, and then figure out how to move the wall further out.

A plan for stress testing should be developed early in the project, because it often helps to clarify exactly what is expected. Is two seconds for a web page request a miserable failure or a smashing success? Is 500 concurrent users enough? That, of course, depends, but one must know the answer when designing the system that answers the request. The stress test needs to model reality well enough to be useful. It isn't really possible to simulate 500 erratic and unpredictable humans using a system concurrently very easily, but one can at least create 500 simulations and try to model some part of what they might do.

46   [1] "to hit"

In stress testing, start out with a light load and load the system along some dimension—such as input rate or input size—until you hit the wall. If the wall is too close to satisfy your needs, figure out which resource is the bottleneck (there is usually a dominant one.) Is it memory, processor, I/O, network bandwidth, or data contention? Then figure out how you can move the wall. Note that moving the wall, that is, increasing the maximum load the system can handle, might not help or might actually hurt the performance of a lightly loaded system. Usually performance under heavy load is more important than performance under a light load.

You may have to get visibility into several different dimensions to build up a mental model of it; no single technique is sufficient. For instance, logging often gives a good idea of the wall-clock time between two events in the system, but unless carefully constructed, doesn't give visibility into memory utilization or even data structure size. Similarly, in a modern system, a number of computers and many software systems may be cooperating. Particularly when you are hitting the wall (that is, the performance is non-linear in the size of the input) these other software systems may be a bottleneck. Visibility into these systems, even if only measuring the processor load on all participating machines, can be very helpful.

Knowing where the wall is is essential not only to moving the wall, but also to providing predictability so that the business can be managed effectively.

How to Balance Brevity and Abstraction

Abstraction is key to programming. You should carefully choose how abstract you need to be. Beginning programmers in their enthusiasm often create more abstraction than is really useful. One sign of this is if you create classes that don't really contain any code and don't really do anything except serve to abstract something. The attraction of this is understandable but the value of code brevity must be measured against the value of abstraction. Occasionally, one sees a mistake made by enthusiastic idealists: at the start of the project a lot of classes are defined that seem wonderfully abstract and one may speculate that they will handle every eventuality that may arise. As the project progresses and fatigue sets in, the code itself becomes messy. Function bodies become longer than they should be. The empty classes are a burden to document that is ignored when under pressure. The final result would have been better if the energy spent on abstraction had been spent on keeping things short and simple. This is a form of *speculative programming*. I strongly recommend the article „Succinctness is Power" by Paul Graham[PGSite].

There is a certain dogma associated with useful techniques such as *information hiding* and *object oriented programming* that are sometimes taken too far. These techniques let one code abstractly and anticipate change. I personally think, however, that you should not produce much speculative code. For example, it is an accepted style to hide an integer variable on an object behind mutators and accessors, so that the variable itself is not exposed, only the little interface to it. This does allow the implementation of that variable to be changed without affecting the calling code, and is perhaps appropriate to a library writer who must publish a very stable API. But I don't think the benefit of this outweighs the cost of the wordiness of it when my team owns the calling code and hence can recode the caller as easily as the called. Four or five extra lines of code is a heavy price to pay for this speculative benefit.

Portability poses a similar problem. Should code be portable to a different computer, compiler, software system or platform, or simply easily ported? I think a non-portable, short-and-easily-ported piece of code is better than a long portable one. It is relatively easy and certainly a good idea to confine non-portable code to designated areas, such as a class that makes database queries that are specific to a given DBMS.

How to Learn New Skills

Learning new skills, especially non-technical ones, is the greatest fun of all. Most companies would have better morale if they understood how much this motivates programmers.

Humans learn by doing. Book-reading and class-taking are useful. But could you have any respect for a programmer who had never written a program? To learn any skill, you have to put yourself in a forgiving position where you can exercise that skill. When learning a new programming language, try to do a small project with it before you have to do a large project. When learning to manage a software project, try to manage a small one first.

A good mentor is no replacement for doing things yourself, but is a lot better than a book. What can you offer a potential mentor in exchange for their knowledge? At a minimum, you should offer to study hard so their time won't be wasted.

Try to get your boss to let you have formal training, but understand that it often not much better than the same amount of time spent simply playing with the new skill you want to learn. It is, however, easier to ask for training than playtime in our imperfect world, even though a lot of formal training is just sleeping through lectures waiting for the dinner party.

If you lead people, understand how they learn and assist them by assigning them projects that are the right size and that exercise skills they are interested in. Don't forget that the most important skills for a programmer are not the technical ones. Give your people a chance to play and practice courage, honesty, and communication.

Learn to Type

Learn to touch-type. This is an intermediate skill because writing code is so hard that the speed at which you can type is irrelevant and can't put much of a dent in the time it takes to write code, no matter how good you are. However, by the time you are an intermediate programmer you will probably spend a lot of time writing natural language to your colleagues and others. This is a fun test of your commitment; it takes dedicated time that is not much fun to learn something like that. Legend has it that when Michael Tiemann was at MCC people would stand outside his door to listen to the hum generated by his keystrokes which were so rapid as to be indistinguishable.

How to Do Integration Testing

Integration testing is the testing of the integration of various components that have been unit tested. Integration is expensive and it comes out in the testing. You must include time for this in your estimates and your schedule.

Ideally you should organize a project so that there is not a phase at the end where integration must explicitly take place. It is far better to gradually integrate things as they are completed over the course of the project. If it is unavoidable estimate it carefully.

Communication Languages

There are some languages, that is, formally defined syntactic systems, that are not programming languages but communication languages --- they are designed specifically to facillitate communication through standardization. In 2003 the most important of these are UML, XML, and SQL. You should have some familiarity with all of these so that you can communicate well and decide when to use them.

UML is a rich formal system for making drawings that describe designs. It's beauty lines in that is both visual and formal, capable of conveying a great deal of information if both the author and the audience know UML. You need to know about it because designs are sometimes communicated in it. There are very helpful tools for making UML drawings that look very professional. In a lot of cases UML is too formal, and I find myself using a simpler boxes and arrows style for design drawings. But I'm fairly sure UML is at least as good for you as studying Latin.

XML is a standard for defining new standards. It is *not* a solution to data interchange problems, though you sometimes see it presented as if it was. Rather, it is a welcome automation of the most boring part of data interchange, namely, structuring the representation into a linear sequence and parsing back into a structure. It provides some nice type- and correctness-checking, though again only a fraction of what you are likely to need in practice.

50

SQL is a very powerful and rich data query and manipulation language that is not quite a programming language. It has many variations, typically quite product-dependent, which are less important than the standardized core. SQL is the lingua franca of relational databases. You may or may not work in any field that can benefit from an understanding of relational databases, but you should have a basic understanding of them and their syntax and meaning of SQL.

Heavy Tools

As our technological culture progresses, software technology moves from inconceivable, to research, to new products, to standardized products, to widely available and inexpensive products. These heavy tools can pull great loads, but can be intimidating and require a large investment in understanding. The intermediate programmer has to know how to manage them and when they should be used or considered.

To my mind right some of the best heavy tools are:

- Relational Databases,
- Full-text Search Engines,
- Math libraries,
- OpenGL,
- XML parsers, and
- Spreadsheets.

How to analyze data

Data analysis is a process in the early stages of software development, when you examine a business activity and find the requirements to convert it into a software application. This is a formal definition, which may lead you to believe that data analysis is an action that you should better leave to the systems analysts, while you, the programmer, should focus on coding what somebody else has designed. If we follow strictly the software engineering paradigm, it may be correct. Experienced programmers become designers and the sharpest designers become business analysts, thus being entitled to think about all the data requirements and give you a well defined task to carry out. This is not entirely accurate, because data is the core value of every programming activity. Whatever you do in your programs, you are either moving around or modifying data. The business analyst is analyzing the needs in a larger scale, and the software designer is further squeezing such scale so that, when the problem lands on your desk, it seems that all you need to do is to apply clever algorithms and start moving existing data.

Not so.

No matter at which stage you start looking at it, data is the main concern of a well designed application. If you look closely at how a business analyst gets the requirements out of the customer?s requests, you?ll realize that data plays a fundamental role. The analyst creates so called Data Flow Diagrams, where all data sources are identified and the flow of information is shaped. Having clearly defined which data should be part of the system, the designer will shape up the data sources, in terms of database relations, data exchange protocols, and file formats, so that the task is ready to be passed down to the programmer. However, the process is not over yet, because you ? the programmer ? even after this thorough process of data refinement, are required to analyze data to perform the task in the best possible way.

The bottom line of your task is the core message of Niklaus Wirth, the father of several languages. ?Algorithms + Data Structures = Programs.? There is never an algorithm standing alone, doing something to itself. Every algorithm is supposed to do something to at least one piece of data.

Therefore, since algorithms don't spin their wheels in a vacuum, you need to analyze both the data that somebody else has identified for you and the data that is necessary to write down your code. A trivial example will make the matter clearer. You are implementing a search routine for a library. According to your specifications, the user can select books by a combination of genre, author, title, publisher, printing year, and number of pages. The ultimate goal of your routine is to produce a legal SQL statement to search the back-end database. Based on these requirements, you have several choices: check each control in turn, using a „switch" statement, or several „if" ones; make an array of data controls, checking

52

each element to see if it is set; create (or use) an abstract control object from which inherit all your specific controls, and connect them to an event-driven engine. If your requirements include also tuning up the query performance, by making sure that the items are checked in a specific order, you may consider using a tree of components to build your SQL statement.

As you can see, the choice of the algorithm depends on the data you decide to use, or to create. Such decisions can make all the difference between an efficient algorithm and a disastrous one. However, efficiency is not the only concern. You may use a dozen named variables in your code and make it as efficient as it can ever be. But such a piece of code might not be easily maintainable.

Perhaps choosing an appropriate container for your variables could keep the same speed and in addition allow your colleagues to understand the code better when they look at it next year. Furthermore, choosing a well defined data structure may allow them to extend the functionality of your code without rewriting it.

In the long run, your choices of data determines how long your code will survive after you are finished with it.

Let me give you another example, just some more food for thought. Let's suppose that your task is to find all the words in a dictionary with more than three anagrams, where an anagram must be another word in the same dictionary. If you think of it as a computational task, you will end up with an endless effort, trying to work out all the combinations of each word and then comparing it to the other words in the list. However, if you analyze the data at hand, you'll realize that each word may be represented by a record containing the word itself and a sorted array of its letters as ID.

Armed with such knowledge, finding anagrams means just sorting the list on the additional field and picking up the ones that share the same ID. The brute force algorithm may take several days to run, while the smart one is just a matter of a few seconds. Remember this example the next time you are facing an intractable problem.

Team Skills

How to Manage Development Time

To manage development time, maintain a concise and up-to-date project plan. A project plan is an estimate, a schedule, a set of milestones for marking progress, and an assignment of your team or your own time to each task on the estimate. It should also include other things you have to remember to do, such as meeting with the quality assurance people, preparing documentation, or ordering equipment. If you are on a team, the project plan should be a consensual agreement, both at the start and as you go.

The project plan exists to help make decisions, not to show how organized you are. If the project plan is either too long or not up-to-date, it will be useless for making decisions. In reality, these decisions are about individual persons. The plan and your judgment let you decide if you should shift tasks from one person to another. The milestones mark your progress. If you use a fancy project planning tool, do not be seduced into creating a Big Design Up Front (BDUF) for the project, but use it maintain concision and up-to-dateness.

If you miss a milestone, you should take immediate action such as informing your boss that the scheduled completion of that project has slipped by that amount. The estimate and schedule could never have been perfect to begin with; this creates the illusion that you might be able to make up the days you missed in the latter part of the project. You might. But it is just as likely that you have underestimated that part as that you have overestimated it. Therefore the scheduled completion of the project has already slipped, whether you like it or not.

Make sure you plan includes time for: internal team meetings, demos, documentation, scheduled periodic activities, integration testing, dealing with outsiders, sickness, vacations, maintenance of existing products, and maintenance of the development environment. The project plan can serve as a way to give outsiders or your boss a view into what you or your team is doing. For this reason it should be short and up-to-date.

How to Manage Third-Party Software Risks

A project often depends on software produced by organizations that it does not control. There are great risks associated with third party software that must be recognized by everyone involved.

Never, ever, rest any hopes on *vapor. Vapor* is any alleged software that has been promised but is not yet available. This is the surest way to go out of business. It is unwise to be merely skeptical of a software company's promise to release a certain product with a certain feature at a certain date; it is far wiser to ignore it completely and forget you ever heard it. Never let it be written down in any documents used by your company.

If third-party software is not vapor, it is still risky, but at least it is a risk that can be tackled. If you are considering using third-party software, you should devote energy early on to evaluating it. People might not like to hear that it will take two weeks or two months to evaluate each of three products for suitability, but it has to be done as early as possible. The cost of integrating cannot be accurately estimated without a proper evaluation.

Understanding the suitability of existing third party software for a particular purpose is very tribal knowledge. It is very subjective and generally resides in experts. You can save a lot of time if you can find those experts. Often times a project will depend on a third-party software system so completely that if the integration fails the project will fail. Express risks like that clearly in writing in the schedule. Try to have a contingency plan, such as another system that can be used or the ability to write the functionality yourself if the risk can't be removed early. Never let a schedule depend on vapor.

How to Manage Consultants

Use consultants, but don't rely on them. They are wonderful people and deserve a great deal of respect. Since they get to see a lot of different projects, they often know more about specific technologies and even programming techniques than you will. The best way to use them is as educators in-house that can teach by example.

55

However, they usually cannot become part of the team in the same sense that regular employees are, if only because you may not have enough time to learn their strengths and weaknesses. Their financial commitment is much lower. They can move more easily. They may have less to gain if the company does well. Some will be good, some will be average, and some will be bad, but hopefully your selection of consultants will not be as careful as your selection of employees, so you will get more bad ones.

If consultants are going to write code, you must review it carefully as you go along. You cannot get to the end of the a project with the risk of a large block of code that has not been reviewed. This is true of all team members, really, but you will usually have more knowledge of the team members closer to you.

How to Communicate the Right Amount

Carefully consider the cost of a meeting; it costs *its duration multiplied by the number of participants*. Meetings are sometimes necessary, but smaller is usually better. The quality of communication in small meetings is better, and less time overall is wasted. If any one person is bored at a meeting take this as a sing, that the meeting should be smaller.

Everything possible should be done to encourage informal communication. More useful work is done during lunches with colleagues than during any other time. It is a shame that more companies do not recognize nor support this fact.

How to Disagree Honestly and Get Away with It

Disagreement is a great opportunity to make a good decision, but it should be handled delicately. Hopefully you feel that you have expressed your thoughts adequately and been heard before the decision is made. In that case there is nothing more to say, and you should decide whether you will stand behind the decision even though you disagree with it. If you can support this decision even though you disagree, say so. This shows how valuable you are because you are independent and are not a yes-man, but respectful of the decision and a team player.

Sometimes a decision that you disagree with will be made when the decision makers did not have the full benefit of you opinion. You should then evaluate whether to raise the issue on the basis of the benefit to the company or tribe. If it is a small mistake in your opinion, it may not be worth reconsidering. If it is a large mistake in you opinion, then of course you must present an argument.

Usually, this is not a problem. In some stressful circumstances and with some personality types this can lead to things being taken personally. For instance, some very good programmers lack the confidence needed to challenge a decision even when they have good reason to believe it is wrong. In the worst of circumstances the decision maker is insecure and takes it as a personal challenge to their authority. It is best to remember that in such circumstances people react with the reptilian part of their brains. You should present your argument in private, and try to show how new knowledge changes the basis on which the decision was made. Whether the decision is reversed or not, you must remember that you will never be able to say 'I told you so!' since the alternate decision was fully explored.

Judgement

How to Tradeoff Quality Against Development Time

Software development is always a compromise between what the project does and getting the project done. But you may be asked to tradeoff quality to speed the deployment of a project in a way that offends your engineering sensibilities or business sensibilities. For example, you may be asked to do something that is a poor software engineering practice and that will lead to a lot of maintenance problems.

If this happens your first responsibility is to inform your team and to clearly explain the cost of the decrease in quality. After all, your understanding of it should be much better than your boss's understanding. Make it clear what is being lost and what is being gained, and at what cost the lost ground will be regained in the next cycle. In this, the visibility provided by a good project plan should be helpful. If the quality tradeoff affects the quality assurance effort, point that out (both to your boss and quality assurance people). If the quality tradeoff will lead to more bugs being reported after the quality assurance period, point that out.

If she still insists you should try to isolate the shoddiness into particular components that you can plan to rewrite or improve in the next cycle. Explain this to your team so that they can plan for it.

NinjaProgrammer at Slashdot sent in this gem:

> Remember that a good *design* will be resillient against poor code implementations. If good interfaces and abstractions exist throughout the code, then the eventual rewrites will be far more painless. If it is hard to write clear code that is hard to fix, consider what is wrong with the core design that is causing this.

How to Manage Software System Dependence

Modern software systems tend to depend on a large number of components that may not be directly under your control. This increases productivity through synergy and reuse. However, each component brings with it some problems:

- How will you fix bugs in the component?
- Does the component restrict you to particular hardware or software systems?
- What will you do if the component fails completely?

It is always best to encapsulate the component in some way so that it is isolated and so that it can be swapped out. If the component proves to be completely unworkable, you may be able to get a different one, but you may have to write your own. Encapsulation is not portability, but it makes porting easier, which is almost as good.

Having the source code for a component decreases the risk by a factor of four. With source code, you can evaluate it easier, debug it easier, find workarounds easier, and make fixes easier. If you make fixes, you should give them to the owner of the component and get the fixes incorporated into an official release; otherwise you will uncomfortably have to maintain an unofficial version .

58

How to Decide if Software is Too Immature

Using software other people wrote is one of the most effective ways to quickly build a solid system. It should not be discouraged, but the risks associated with it must be examined.

One of the biggest risks is the period of bugginess and near inoperability that is often associated with software before it matures, through usage, into a usable product. Before you consider integrating with a software system, whether created in house or by a third party, it is very important to consider if it is really mature enough to be used. Here are ten questions you should ask yourself about it:

1. Is it vapor? (Promises are very immature).

2. Is there an accessible body of lore about the software?

3. Are you the first user?

4. Is there a strong incentive for continuation?

5. Has it had a maintenance effort?

6. Will it survive defection of the current maintainers?

7. Is there a seasoned alternative at least half as good?

8. Is it known to your tribe or company?

9. Is it desirable to your tribe or company?

10. Can you hire people to work on it even if it is bad?

A little consideration of these criteria demonstrates the great value of well-established free software and open-source software in reducing risk to the entrepreneur

How to Make a Buy vs. Build Decision

An entrepreneurial company or project that is trying to accomplish something with software has to constantly make so-called buy vs. build decisions. This turn of phrase is unfortunate in two ways: it seems to ignore open-source and free software which is not necessarily *bought*. Even more importantly, it should perhaps be called an *obtain and integrate* vs. *build here and integrate* decision because the cost of integration must be considered. This requires a great combination of business, management, and engineering savvy.

- How well do your needs match those for which it was designed?
- What portion of what you buy will you need?
- What is the cost of evaluating the integration?
- What is the cost of integration?
- What is the cost of evaluating the integration?
- Will buying increase or decrease long term maintenance costs?
- Will building it put you in a business position you don't want to be in?

You should think twice before building something that is big enough to serve as the basis for an entire other business. Such ideas are often proposed by bright and optimistic people that will have a lot to contribute to your team. If their idea is compelling, you may wish to change your business plan; but do not invest in a solution bigger than your own business without conscious thought.

After considering these questions, you should perhaps prepare two draft project plans, one for building and one for buying. This will force you to consider the integration costs. You should also consider the long term maintenance costs of both solutions. To estimate the integration costs, you will have to do a thorough evaluation of the software before you buy it. If you can't evaluate it, you will assume an unreasonable risk in buying it and you should decide against buying that particular product. If there are several buy decisions under consideration, some energy will have to be spent evaluating each.

60

How to Grow Professionally

Assume responsibility in excess of your authority. Play the role that you desire. Express appreciation for people's contribution to the success of the larger organization, as well as things that help you personally.

If you want to become a team leader, instigate the formation of consensus. If you want to become a manager, take responsibility for the schedule. You can usually do this comfortably while working with a leader or a manager, since this frees them up to take greater responsibility. If that is too much to try, do it a little at a time.

Evaluate yourself. If you want to become a better programmer, ask someone you admire how you can become like them. You can also ask your boss, who will know less but have a greater impact on your career.

Plan ways to learn new skills, both the trivial technical kind, like learning a new software system, and the hard social kind, like writing well, by integrating them into your work.

How to Evaluate Interviewees

Evaluating potential employees is not given the energy it deserves. A bad hire, like a bad marriage, is terrible. A significant portion of everyone's energy should be devoted to recruitment, though this is rarely done.

There are different interviewing styles. Some are torturous, designed to put the candidate under a great deal of stress. This serves a very valuable purpose of possibly revealing character flaws and weaknesses under stress. Candidates are no more honest with interviewers than they are with themselves, and the human capacity for self-deception is astonishing.

You should, at a minimum, give the candidate the equivalent of an oral examination on the technical skills for two hours. With practice, you will be able to quickly cover what they know and quickly retract from what they don't know to mark out the boundary. Interviewees will respect this. I have several times heard interviewees say that the quality of the examination was one of their motivations for choosing a company. Good

61

people want to be hired for their skills, not where they worked last or what school they went to or some other inessential characteristic.

In doing this, you should also evaluate their ability to learn, which is far more important than what they know. You should also watch for the whiff of brimstone that is given off by difficult people. You may be able to recognize it by comparing notes after the interview, but in the heat of the interview it is hard to recognize. How well people communicate and work with people is more important than being up on the latest programming language.

A reader has had good luck using a 'take-home' test for interviewees. This has the advantage that can uncover the interviewee that can present themselves well but can't really code --- and there are many such people. I personally have not tried this technique, but it sounds sensible.

Finally, interviewing is also a process of selling. You should be selling your company or project to the candidate. However, you are talking to a programmer, so don't try to color the truth. Start off with the bad stuff, then finish strong with the good stuff.

How to Know When to Apply Fancy Computer Science

There is a body of knowledge about algorithms, data structures, mathematics, and other gee-whiz stuff that most programmers know about but rarely use. In practice, this wonderful stuff is too complicated and generally unnecessary. There is no point in improving an algorithm when most of your time is spent making inefficient database calls, for instance. An unfortunate amount of programming consists of getting systems to talk to each other and using very simple data structures to build a nice user interface.

When is high technology the appropriate technology? When should you crack a book to get something other than a run-of-the-mill algorithm? It is sometimes useful to do this but it should be evaluated carefully.

The three most important considerations for the potential computer science technique are:

- Is it well encapsulated so that the risk to other systems is low and the overall increase in complexity and maintenance cost is low?
- Is the benefit startling (for example, a factor of two in a mature system or a factor of ten in a new system)?
- Will you be able to test and evaluate it effectively?

If a well-isolated algorithm that uses a slightly fancy algorithm can decrease hardware cost or increase performance by a factor of two across an entire system, then it would be criminal not to consider it. One of the keys to arguing for such an approach is to show that the risk is really quite low, since the proposed technology has probably been well studied, the only issue is the risk of integration. Here a programmer's experience and judgment can truly synergize with the fancy technology to make integration easy.

How to Talk to Non-Engineers

Engineers and programmers in particular are generally recognized by popular culture as being different from other people. This implies that other people are different from us. This is worth bearing in mind when communicating with non-engineers; you should always understand the audience.

Non-engineers are smart, but not as grounded in creating technical things as we are. We make things. They sell things and handle things and count things and manage things, but they are not experts on making things. They are not as good at working together on teams as engineers are (there are no doubt exceptions.) Their social skills are generally as good as or better than engineers in non-team environments, but their work does not always demand that they practice the kind of intimate, precise communication and careful subdivisions of tasks that we do.

Non-engineers may be too eager to please and they may be intimidated by you. Just like us, they may say 'yes' without really meaning it to please you or because they are a little scared of you, and then not stand behind their words.

Non-programmers can understand technical things but they do not have the thing that is so hard even for us—technical judgment. They do understand how technology works, but they cannot understand why a certain approach would take three months and another one three days. (After all, programmers are anecdotally horrible at this kind of estimation as well.) This represents a great opportunity to synergize with them.

When talking to your team you will, without thinking, use a sort of shorthand, an abbreviated language that is effective because you will have much shared experience about technology in general and your product in particular. It takes some effort not to use this shorthand with those that don't have that shared experience, especially when members of your own team are present. This vocabulary create a wall between you and those that do not share it, and, even worse, wastes their time.

With your team, the basic assumptions and goals do not need to be restated often, and most conversation focuses on the details. With outsiders, it must be the other way around. They may not understand things you take for granted. Since you take them for granted and don't repeat them, you can leave a conversation with an outsider thinking that you understand each other when really there is a large misunderstanding. You should assume that you will miscommunicate and watch carefully to find this miscommunication. Try to get them to summarize or paraphrase what you are saying to make sure they understand. If you have the opportunity to meet with them often, spend a little bit of time asking if you you are communicating effectively, and how you can do it better. If there is a problem in communication, seek to alter your own practices before becoming frustrated with theirs.

I love working with non-engineers. It provides great opportunities to learn and to teach. You can often lead by example, in terms of the clarity of your communication. Engineers are trained to bring order out of chaos, to bring clarity out of confusion, and non-engineers like this about us. Because we have technical judgment and can usually understand business issues, we can often find a simple solution to a problem.

Often non-engineers propose solutions that they think will make it easier on us out of kindness and a desire to do the right thing, when in fact a much better overall solution exists which can only be seen by synergizing the outsiders view with your technical judgment. I personally like Extreme Programming because it addresses this inefficiency; by marrying the estimation quickly to the idea, it makes it easier to find the idea that is the best combination of cost and benefit.

Part 3
Advanced

Technological Judgment

How to Tell the Hard From the Impossible

It is our job to do the hard and discern the impossible. From the point of view of most working programmers, something is impossible if either it cannot be grown from a simple system or it cannot be estimated. By this definition what is called research is impossible. A large volume of mere work is hard, but not necessarily impossible.

The distinction is not facetious because you may very well be asked to do what is practically impossible, either from a scientific point of view or a software engineering point of view. It then becomes your job to help the entrepreneur find a reasonable solution which is *merely hard* and gets most of what they wanted. A solution is merely hard when it can be confidently scheduled and the risks are understood.

It is impossible to satisfy a vague requirement, such as 'Build a system that will compute the most attractive hair style and color for any person.' If the requirement can be made more crisp, it will often become merely hard, such as 'Build a system to compute an attractive hair style and color for a person, allow them to preview it and make changes, and have the customer satisfaction based on the original styling be so great that we make a lot of money.' If there is not crisp definition of success, you will not succeed.

How to Utilize Embedded Languages

Embedding a programming language into a system has an almost erotic fascination to a programmer. It is one of the most creative acts that can be performed. It makes the system tremendously powerful. It allows you to exercise her most creative and Promethean skills. It makes the system into your friend.

The best text editors in the world all have embedded languages. This can be used to the extent that the intended audience can master the language. Of course, use of the language can be made optional, as it is in text editors, so that initiates can use it and no one else has to.

I and many other programmers have fallen into the trap of creating special purpose embedded languages. I fell into it twice. There already exist many languages designed specifically to be embedded languages. You should think twice before creating a new one.

The real question to ask oneself before embedding a language is: Does this work with or against the culture of my audience? If you intended audience is exclusively non-programmers, how will it help? If your intended audience is exclusively programmers, would they prefer an applications programmers interface (API)? And what language will it be? Programmers don't want to learn a new language that is narrowly used; but if it meshes with their culture they will not have to spend much time learning it. It is a joy to create a new language. But we should not let that blind us to the needs of the user. Unless you have some truly original needs and ideas, why not use an existing language so that you can leverage the familiarity users already have with it?

Choosing Languages

The solitary programmer that loves his work (a hacker) can choose the best language for the task. Most working programmers have very little control of the language they will use. Generally, this issue is dictated by pointy-haired bosses who are making a political decision, rather than a technological decision, and lack the courage to promote an unconventional tool even when they know, often with firsthand knowledge, that the less accepted tool is best. In other cases the very real benefit of unity among the team, and to some extent with a larger community, precludes choice on the part of the individual. Often managers are driven by the need to be able to hire programmers with experience in a given language. No doubt they are serving what they perceive to be the best interests of the project or company, and must be respected for that. However, I personally believe this the most wasteful and erroneous common practice you are likely to encounter.

But of course, things are never one-dimensional. Even if a core language is mandated and beyond your control, it is often the case that tools and other programs can and should be written in a different language. If a language is to be embedded (and you should always consider it!) the choice of language will depend a lot on the culture of the users. One should take advantage of this to serve your company or project by using the best language for the job, and in so doing make work more interesting.

Programming languages should really be called notations in that learning one is not at all as difficult as learning a natural language. To beginners and to some outsiders „learning a new language" seems a daunting task; but after you have three under your belt it's really just a question of becoming familiar with the available libraries. One tends to think of a large system that has components in three or four languages as a messy hodgepodge; but I argue that such a system is in many cases stronger than a one-language system in several ways:

- There is necessarily loose coupling between the components that are written in different notations (though maybe not clean interfaces),
- You can evolve to a new language/platform easily by rewriting each component individually,
- Its possible that some of the modules are actually up-to-date.

Some of these effects may only be psychological; but psychology matters. In the end the costs of language tyranny outweigh any advantage that it provides.

Compromising Wisely

How to Fight Schedule Pressure

Time-to-market pressure is the pressure to deliver a good product quickly. It is good because it reflects a financial reality, and is healthy up to a point. Schedule pressure is the pressure to deliver something faster than it can be delivered and it is wasteful, unhealthy, and all too common.

Schedule pressure exists for several reasons. The people who task programmers do not fully appreciate what a strong work ethic we have and how much fun it is to be a programmer. Perhaps because they project their own behavior onto us, they believe that asking for it sooner will make us work harder to get it there sooner. This is probably actually true, but the effect is very small, and the damage is very great. Additionally, they have no visibility into what it really takes to produce software. Not being able to see it, and not be able to create it themselves, the only thing they can do is see time-to-market pressure and fuss at programmers about it.

The key to fighting schedule pressure is simply to turn it into time-to-market pressure. The way to do this to give visibility into the relationship between the available labor and the product. Producing an honest, detailed, and most of all, *understandable* estimate of all the labor involved is the best way to do this. It has the added advantage of allowing good management decisions to be made about possible functionality tradeoffs.

The key insight that the estimate must make plain is that labor is an almost incompressible fluid. You can't pack more into a span of time anymore than you can pack more water into a container over and above that container's volume. In a sense, a programmer should never say 'no', but rather to say 'What will you give up to get that thing you want?' The effect of producing clear estimates will be to increase the respect for programmers. This is how other professionals behave. Programmers' hard work will be visible. Setting an unrealistic schedule will also be painfully obvious to everyone. Programmers cannot be hoodwinked. It is disrespectful and demoralizing to ask them to do something unrealistic. Extreme Programming amplifies this and builds a process around it; I hope that every reader will be lucky enough to use it.

How to Understand the User

It is your duty to understand the user, and to help your boss understand the user. Because the user is not as intimately involved in the creation of your product as you are, they behave a little differently:

- The user generally makes short pronouncements.
- The user has their own job; they will mainly think of small improvements in your product, not big improvements.
- The user can't have a vision that represents the complete body of your product users.

71

It is your duty to give them what they really want, not what they say they want. It is however, better to propose it to them and get them to agree that your proposal is what they really want before you begin, but they may not have the vision to do this. Your confidence in your own ideas about this should vary. You must guard against both arrogance and false modesty in terms of knowing what the customer really wants. Programmers are trained to design and create. Market researchers are trained to figure out what people want. These two kinds of people, or two modes of thought in the same person, working harmoniously together give the best chance of formulating the correct vision.

The more time you spend with users the better you will be able to understand what will really be successful. You should try to test your ideas against them as much as you can. You should eat and drink with them if you can.

Guy Kawasaki[Rules] has emphasized the importance of *watching* what your users do in addition to listening to them.

I believe contractors and consultants often have tremendous problems getting their clients to clarify in their own minds what they really want. If you intend to be a consultant, I suggest you choose your clients based on their clear-headedness as well as their pocketbooks.

How to Get a Promotion

To be promoted to a role, act out that role first.

To get promoted to a title, find out what is expected of that title and do that.

To get a pay raise, negotiate armed with information.

If you feel like you are past due for a promotion, talk to your boss about it. Ask them explicitly what you need to do to get promoted, and try to do it. This sounds trite, but often times your perception of what you need to do will differ considerably from your boss's. Also this will pin your boss down in some ways.

Most programmers probably have an exaggerated sense of their relative abilities in some ways—after all, we can't all be in the top 10%! However, I have seem some people who were seriously unappreciated. One cannot expect everyone's evaluation to perfectly match reality at all times, but I think people are generally moderately fair, with one caveat: you cannot be appreciated without visibility into your work. Sometimes, do to happenstance or personal habits, someone will not be noticed much. Working from home a lot or being geographically separated from your team and boss makes this especially difficult.

Serving Your Team

How to Develop Talent

Nietschze exaggerated when he said[Stronger]:

What does not destroy me, makes me stronger.

Your greatest responsibility is to your team. You should know each of them well. You should stretch your team, but not overburden them. You should usually talk to them about the way they are being stretched. If they buy in to it, they will be well motivated. On each project, or every other project, try to stretch them in both a way that they suggest and a way that you think will be good for them. Stretch them not by giving them more work, but by giving them a new skill or better yet a new role to play on the team.

You should allow people (including yourself) to fail occasionally and should plan for some failure in your schedule. If there is never any failure, there can be no sense of adventure. If there are not occasional failures, you are not trying hard enough. When someone fails, you should be as gentle as you can with them while not treating them as though they had succeeded.

Try to get each team member to buy in and be well motivated. Ask each of them explicitly what they need to be well-motivated if they are not. You may have to leave them dissatisfied, but you should know what everybody desires.

73

You can't give up on someone who is intentionally not carrying their share of the load because of low morale or dissatisfaction and just let them be slack. You must try to get them well-motivated and productive. As long as you have the patience, keep this up. When your patience is exhausted, fire them. You cannot allow someone who is intentionally working below their level to remain on the team, since it is not fair to the team.

Make it clear to the strong members of your team that you think they are strong by saying so in public. Praise should be public and criticism private.

The strong members of the team will naturally have more difficult tasks than the weak members of the team. This is perfectly natural and nobody will be bothered by it as long as everyone works hard.

It is an odd fact that is not reflected in salaries that a good programmer is more productive than 10 bad programmers. This creates a strange situation. It will often be true that you could move faster if your weak programmers would just get out of the way. If you did this you would in fact make more progress in the short term. However, your tribe would lose some important benefits, namely the training of the weaker members, the spreading of tribal knowledge, and the ability to recover from the loss of the strong members. The strong must be gentle in this regard and consider the issue from all angles.

You can often give the stronger team members challenging, but carefully delineated, tasks.

How to Choose What to Work On

You balance your personal needs against the needs of the team in choosing what aspect of a project to work on. You should do what you are best at, but try to find a way to stretch yourself not by taking on more work but by exercising a new skill. Leadership and communication skills are more important than technical skills. If you are very strong, take on the hardest or riskiest task, and do it as early as possible in the project to decrease risk.

74

How to Get the Most From Your Teammates

To get the most from your teammates, develop a good team spirit and try to keep every individual both personally challenged and personally engaged.

To develop team spirit, corny stuff like logoized clothing and parties are good, but not as good as personal respect. If everyone respects everyone else, nobody will want to let anybody down. Team spirit is created when people make sacrifices for the team and think in terms of the good of the team before their own personal good. As a leader, you can't ask for more than you give yourself in this respect.

One of the keys to team leadership is to facilitate consensus so that everyone has buy in. This occasionally means allowing your teammates to be wrong. That is, if it does not harm the project too much, you must let some of your team do things their own way, based on consensus, even if you believe with great confidence it is the wrong thing to do. When this happens, don't agree, simply disagree openly and accept the consensus. Don't sound hurt, or like you're being forced into it, simply state that you disagree but think the consensus of the team is more important. This will often cause them to backtrack. Don't insist that they go through with their initial plan if they do backtrack.

If there is an individual who will not consent after you have discussed the issues from all appropriate sides, simply assert that you have to make a decision and that is what your decision is. If there is a way to judge if your decision will be wrong or if it is later shown to be wrong, switch as quickly as you can and recognize the persons who were right.

Ask your team, both as a group and individually, what they think would create team spirit and make for an effective team.

Praise frequently rather than lavishly. Especially praise those who disagree with you when they are praiseworthy. Praise in public and criticize in private; with one exception: sometimes growth or the correction of a fault can't be praised without drawing embarrassing attention to the original fault, so that growth should be praised in private.

How to Divide Problems Up

It's fun to take a software project and divide it up into tasks that will be performed by individuals. This should be done early. Sometimes managers like to think that an estimate can be made without consideration of the individuals that will perform the work. This is impossible since the productivity of individuals varies so widely. Who has particular knowledge about a component also constantly changes and can have an order of magnitude effect on performance.

Just as a composer considers the timbre of the instrument that will play a part or the coach of an athletic team considers the strengths of each player, the experienced team leader will not usually be able to separate the division of the project into tasks from the team members to which they will be assigned. This is part of the reason that a high-performing team should not be broken up.

There is a certain danger in this given that people will become bored as they build upon their strengths and never improve their weaknesses or learn new skills. However, specialization is a very useful productivity tool when not overused.

How to Handle Boring Tasks

Sometimes it is not possible to avoid boring tasks that are critical to the success of the company or the project. These tasks can really hurt the morale of those that have to do them. The best technique for dealing with this is to invoke or promote Larry Wall's programmer's virtue of Laziness. Try to find some way to get the computer to do the task for you or to help your teammates do this. Working for a week on a program to do a task that will take a week to do by hand has the great advantage of being more educational and sometimes more repeatable.

If all else fails, apologize to those who have to do the boring task, but under no circumstances allow them to do it alone. At a minimum assign a team of two to do the work and promote healthy teamwork to get the task done.

76

How to Gather Support for a Project

To gather support for a project, create and communicate a vision that demonstrates real value to the organization as a whole. Attempt to let others share in your vision creation. This gives them a reason to support you and gives you the benefit of their ideas. Individually recruit key supporters for your project. Wherever possible, show, don't tell. If possible, construct a prototype or a mockup to demonstrate your ideas. A prototype is always powerful but in software it is far superior to any written description.

How to Grow a System

The seed of a tree contains the idea of the adult but does not fully realize the form and potency of the adult. The embryo grows. It becomes larger. It looks more like the adult and has more of the uses. Eventually it bears fruit. Later, it dies and its body feeds other organisms.

We have the luxury of treating software like that. A bridge is not like that; there is never a baby bridge, but merely an unfinished bridge. Bridges are a lot simpler than software.

It is good to think of software as growing, because it allows us to make useful progress before we have a perfect mental image. We can get feedback from users and use that to correct the growth. Pruning off weak limbs is healthful.

The programmer must design a finished system that can be delivered and used. But the advanced programmer must do more. You must design a growth path that ends in the finished system. It is your job to take a germ of an idea and build a path that takes it as smoothly as possible into a useful artifact.

To do this, you must visualize the end result and communicate it in a way that the engineering team can get excited about. But you must also communicate to them a path that goes from wherever they are now to where they want to be with no large leaps. The tree must stay alive the whole time; it cannot be dead at one point and resurrected later.

77

This approach is captured in spiral development. Milestones that are never too far apart are used to mark progress along the path. In the ultra-competitive environment of business, it is best if the milestones can be released and make money as early as possible, even if they are far away from a well-designed endpoint. One of the programmer's jobs is to balance the immediate payoff against future payoff by wisely choosing a growth path expressed in milestones.

The advanced programmer has the triple responsibility of growing software, teams, and persons.

A reader, Rob Hafernik, sent in this comment on this section that I can do no better than to quote in full:

> *I think you under-emphasize the importance here. It's not just systems, but algorithms, user interfaces, data models, and so on. It's absolutely vital as you work on a large system to have measurable progress toward intermediate goals. Nothing is as bad as the special horror of getting down to the end and discovering that the whole thing just isn't going to work (look at the recent debacle of the Voter News System). I would even go further and state it as a law of nature: no large, complex system can be implemented from scratch, it can only be evolved from a simple system to a complex system in a series of intentional steps.*

To which one can only reply Fiat lux!

How to Communicate Well

To communicate well, you have to recognize how hard it is. It is a skill unto itself. It is made harder by the fact that the persons with whom you have to communicate are flawed. They do not work hard at understanding you. They speak poorly and write poorly. They are often overworked or bored, and, at a minimum, somewhat focused on their own work rather than the larger issues you may be addressing. One of the advantages of taking classes and practicing writing, public speaking, and listening is that if you become good at it you can more readily see where problems lie and how to correct them.

78

The programmer is a social animal whose survival depends on communication with her team. The advanced programmer is a social animal whose satisfaction depends on communication with people outside her team.

The programmer brings order out of chaos. One interesting way to do this is to initiate a proposal of some kind outside the team. This can be done in a strawman or white-paper format or just verbally. This leadership has the tremendous advantage of setting the terms of the debate. It also exposes you to criticism, and worse, rejection and neglect. The advanced programmer must be prepared to accept this, because she has a unique power and therefore a unique responsibility. Entrepreneurs who are not programmers need programmers to provide leadership in some ways. Programmers are the part of the bridge between ideas and reality that rests on reality.

I haven't mastered communicating well, but what I'm currently trying is what I think of a four-pronged approach: After I have my ideas in order and am fully prepared, I try to speak verbally, hand people a white-paper (on real paper, as well as electronically) show them a demo, and then patiently repeat this process. I think a lot of times we are not patient enough in this kind of difficult communication. You should not be disheartened if your ideas are not immediately accepted. If you have invested energy in there preparation, no one will think poorly of you for it.

How to Tell People Things They Don't Want to Hear

You will often have to tell people things that will make them uncomfortable. Remember that you are doing this for a reason. Even if nothing can be done about the problem, you are telling them as early as possible so they will be well-informed.

The best way to tell someone about a problem is to offer a solution at the same time. The second best way is to appeal to them for help with the problem. If there is a danger that you won't be believed, you should gather some support for your assertion.

One of the most unpleasant and common things you will have to say is, 'The schedule will have to slip.' The conscientious programmer hates to say this, but must say it as early as possible. There is nothing worse than postponing action when a milestone slips, even if the only action is to inform everyone. In doing this, it is better to do it as a team, at least in spirit, if not physically. You will want your team's input on both where you stand and what can be done about it, and the team will have to face the consequences with you.

How to Deal with Managerial Myths

The word *myth* sometimes means fiction. But it has a deeper connotation. It also means a story of religious significance that explains the universe and mankind's relationship to it. Managers tend to forget what they learned as programmers and believe in certain myths. It would be as rude and unsuccessful to try to convince them these myths are false as to try to disillusion a devoutly religious person of their beliefs. For that reason, you should recognize these beliefs as myths:

- More documentation is always better. (They want it, but they don't want you to spend any time on it.)
- Programmers can be equated. (Programmers vary by an order of magnitude.)
- Resources can be added to a late project to speed it. (The cost of communication with the new persons is almost always more taxing than helpful.)
- It is possible to estimate software development reliably. (It is not even theoretically possible.)
- Programmers' productivity can be measured in terms of some simple metric, like lines of code. (If succinctness is power, lines of code are bad, not good.)

If you have an opportunity, you can try to explain these things, but don't feel bad if you have no success and don't damage your reputation by confronting these myths belligerently. Each of these myths reinforces the manager's idea that they have some actual control over what is going on. The truth is that managers facilitate if they are good, and impede if they are bad.

80

How to Deal with Organizational Chaos

There are often brief periods of great organizational chaos, such as layoffs, buyouts, ipos, firings, new hirings, and so on. These are unsettling to everyone, but perhaps a little less unsettling to the programmer whose personal self-esteem is founded in capacity rather than in position. Organizational chaos is a great opportunity for programmers to exercise their magic power. I've saved this for last because it is a deep tribal secret. If you are not a programmer, please stop reading now.

Engineers have the power to create and sustain.

Non-engineers can order people around but, in a typical software company, can create and sustain nothing without engineers, just as engineers typically cannot sell a product or manage a business effectively. This power is proof against almost all of the problems associated with temporary organizational mayhem. When you have it you should ignore the chaos completely and carry on as if nothing is happening. You may, of course, get fired, but if that happens you can probably get a new job because of the magic power. More commonly, some stressed-out person who does not have the magic power will come into your cube and tell you to do something stupid. If you are really sure that it is stupid, it is best to smile and nod until they go away and then carry on doing what you know is best for the company.

If you are a leader, tell your people to do the same thing and tell them to ignore what anybody else tells them. This course of action is the best for you personally, and is the best for your company or project.

Glossary

This is a glossary of terms as used in this essay. These do not necessarily have a standardized meaning to other people. Eric S. Raymond has compiled a massive and informative glossary[HackerDict] that rather surprisingly can pleasurably be read cover-to-cover once you can appreciate a fraction of it.

unk-unk
> Slang for unknown-unknown. Problems that cannot presently even be conceptualized that will steal time away from the project and wreck the schedule.

boss
> The person or entity that gives you tasks. In some cases this may be the public at large.

printlining
> The insertion of statements into a program on a strictly temporary basis that output information about the execution of the program for the purpose of debugging.

logging
> The practice of writing a program so that it can produce a configurable output log describing its execution.

divide and conquer
> A technique of top-down design and, importantly, of debugging that is the subdivision of a problem or a mystery into progressively smaller problems or mysteries.

vapor
> Illusionary and often deceptive promises of software that is not yet for sale and, as often as not, will never materialize into anything solid.

boss
> The person who sets your tasks. In some cases, the user is the boss.

tribe
> The people with whom you share loyalty to a common goal.

low-hanging fruit
> Big improvements that cost little.

Entrepreneur

The initiator of projects.

garbage

Objects that are no longer needed that hold memory.

business

A group of people organized for making money.

company

A group of people organized for making money.

tribe

A group of people you share cultural affinity and loyalty with.

scroll blindness

The effect of being unable to find information you need because it is buried in too much other, less interesting information.

wall-clock

Actually time as measured by a clock on a wall, as opposed to CPU time.

bottleneck

The most important limitation in the performance of a system. A constriction that limits performance.

master

A unique piece of information from which all cached copies are derived that serves as the official definition of that data.

heap allocated

Memory can be said to be heap allocated whenever the mechanism for freeing it is complicated.

garbage

Allocated memory that no longer has any useful meaning.

garbage collector

A system for recycling garbage.

memory leak

The unwanted collection of references to objects that prevents garbage collection (or a bug in the garbage collector or memory management system!) that causes the program to gradually increase its memory demands over time.

Extreme Programming

A style of programming emphasizing communication with the customer and automated testing.

hitting the wall

> To run out of a specific resource causing performance to degrade sharply rather than gradually.

speculative programming

> Producing a feature before it is really known if that feature will be useful.

information hiding

> A design principle that seeks to keep things independent and decoupled by using interfaces that expose as little information as possible.

object-oriented programming

> An programming style emphasizing the the management of state inside objects.

communication languages

> A language designed primarily for standardization rather than execution.

boxes and arrows

> A loose, informal style of making diagrams consiting of boxes and arrows drawn between those boxes to show the relationships. This contrast with formal diagram methodologies, such as UML.

lingua franca

> A language so popular as to be a de facto standard for its field, as French was for international diplomacy at one time.

buy vs. build

> An adjective describing a choice between spending money for software or writing it your self.

mere work

> Work that requires little creativity and entails little risk. Mere work can be estimated easily.

programming notation

> A synonym for programming language that emphasizes the mathematical nature of programming language and their relative simplicity compared to natural languages.

strawman

> A document meant to be the starting point of a technical discussion. A strawman may lead to a stickman, tinman, woodman, ironman, etc.

white-paper

An informative document that is often meant to explain or sell a product or idea to an audience different than the programmers of that product or idea.

Appendix A.

Bibliography/Websiteography

Books

[Rules00] Guy Kawasaki, Michelle Moreno, and Gary Kawasaki. 2000. HarperBusiness. *Rules for Revolutionaries: The Capitalist Manifesto for Creating and Marketing New Products and Services*.
[RDev96] Steve McConnell. 1996. Microsoft Press. Redmond, Wash. *Rapid Development: Taming Wild Software Schedules*.
[CodeC93] Steve McConnell. 1993. Microsoft Press. Redmond, Wash. *Code Complete*.
[XP99] Kent Beck. 1999. 0201616416. Addison-Wesley. *Extreme Programming Explained: Embrace Change*.
[PlanXP00] Kent Beck and Martin Fowler. 2000. 0201710919. Addison-Wesley. *Planning Extreme Programming*.
[Prag99] Andrew Hunt, David Thomas, and Ward Cunningham. 1999. 020161622X. Addison-Wesley. *The Pragmatic Programmer: From Journeyman to Master*.
[Stronger] Friedrich Nietzsche. 1889. *Twilight of the Idols, „ Maxims and Arrows“, section 8.*.

Web Sites

[PGSite] Paul Graham. 2002. *Articles on his website: http://www.paulgraham.com/articles.html. All of them, but especially „Beating the Averages“*.
[Hacker] Eric S. Raymond. 2003. *How to Become a Hacker*. http://www.catb.org/~esr/faqs/hacker-howto.html.
[HackDict] Eric S. Raymond. 2003. *The New Hacker Dictionary*. http://catb.org/esr/jargon/jargon.html.
[ExpCS] Edsger W. Dijkstra. 1986. *How Experimental is Computing Science?*. http://www.cs.utexas.edu/users/EWD/ewd09xx/EWD988a.PDF.
[Knife] Edsger W. Dijkstra. 1984. *On a Cultural Gap*. http://www.cs.utexas.edu/users/EWD/ewd09xx/EWD913.PDF .

Appendix B.

History (As Of February, 2003)

Request for Feedback or Extension

Please send me any comments you may have on this essay. I consider all suggestions, many of which have already improved this essay.

I have placed this essay under the GNU Free Documentation License. This license is not specifically designed for essays. Essays are usually intended to be coherent and convincing arguments that are writtien from a single point of view in a single voice. I hope this essay is a short and pleasant read.

I also hope that it is instructive. Although not a textbook, it is broken into many small sections to which new sections can be freely added. If so inclined, you are encouraged to expand upon this essay as you see fit, subject to the provisions of the License.

It may be arrogance to imagine that this document is worthy of extension; but hope springs eternal. I would be joyous if it were extended in the following ways:

- · The addition of a comprehensive reading list to each section,
- · The addition of more and better sections,
- · Translation into other languages, even if only on a subsection-by-subsection basis, and/or
- · Criticism or commentary in-lined into the text.
- · The ability to build into different formats, such as palm formats and better HTML.

If you inform me of your work, I will consider it and may include it in subsequent versions that I produce, subject to the provisions of the License. You may of course produce your own versions of this document without my knowledge, as explained in the License.

Thank you.
Robert L. Read

Original Version

The original version of this document was begun by Robert L. Read in the year 2000 and first published electronically at Samizdat Press(http://Samizdat.mines.edu) in 2002. It is dedicated to the programmers of Hire.com.

After this article was mentioned on Slashdot in 2003, about 75 people sent me email with suggestions and errata. I appreciate them all. There was a lot of duplication, but the following people either made major suggestions or were the first to find a bug that I fixed: Morgan McGuire, David Mason, Tom Moertel, Ninja Programmer (145252) at Slashdot, Ben Vierck, Rob Hafernik, Mark Howe, Pieter Pareit, Brian Grayson, Zed A. Shaw, Steve Benz, Maksim Ioffe, Andrew Wu, David Jeschke, and Tom Corcoran.

Finally I would like to thank Christina Vallery, whose editing and proofreading greatly improved the second draft, and Wayne Allen, who encouraged me to initiate this.

Original Author's Bio

Robert L. Read lives in Austin, Texas, with his wife and two children. He is currently a Principal Engineer at Hire.com, where he has worked for four years. Prior to that he founded 4R Technology, which made a scanner-based image analysis quality control tool for the paper industry. Rob received a PhD from the University of Texas at Austin in 1995 in Computer Science related to database theory. In 1987 he received a BA in Computer Science from Rice University. He has been a paid programmer since the age of 16.

Appendix C.

GNU Free Documentation License

Version 1.2, November 2002

PREAMBLE

The purpose of this License is to make a manual, textbook, or other functional and useful document „free" in the sense of freedom: to assure everyone the effective freedom to copy and redistribute it, with or without modifying it, either commercially or noncommercially. Secondarily, this License preserves for the author and publisher a way to get credit for their work, while not being considered responsible for modifications made by others.

This License is a kind of „copyleft", which means that derivative works of the document must themselves be free in the same sense. It complements the GNU General Public License, which is a copyleft license designed for free software.

We have designed this License in order to use it for manuals for free software, because free software needs free documentation: a free program should come with manuals providing the same freedoms that the software does. But this License is not limited to software manuals; it can be used for any textual work, regardless of subject matter or whether it is published as a printed book. We recommend this License principally for works whose purpose is instruction or reference.

APPLICABILITY AND DEFINITIONS

This License applies to any manual or other work, in any medium, that contains a notice placed by the copyright holder saying it can be distributed under the terms of this License. Such a notice grants a world-wide, royalty-free license, unlimited in duration, to use that work under the conditions stated herein. The „Document", below, refers to any such manual or work. Any member of the public is a licensee, and is addressed as „you". You accept the license if you copy, modify or distribute the work in a way requiring permission under copyright law.

A „Modified Version" of the Document means any work containing the Document or a portion of it, either copied verbatim, or with modifications and/or translated into another language.

A „Secondary Section" is a named appendix or a front-matter section of the Document that deals exclusively with the relationship of the publishers or authors of the Document to the Document's overall subject (or to related matters) and contains nothing that could fall directly within that overall subject. (Thus, if the Document is in part a textbook of mathematics, a Secondary Section may not explain any mathematics.) The relationship could be a matter of historical connection with the subject or with related matters, or of legal, commercial, philosophical, ethical or political position regarding them.

The „Invariant Sections" are certain Secondary Sections whose titles are designated, as being those of Invariant Sections, in the notice that says that the Document is released under this License. If a section does not fit the above definition of Secondary then it is not allowed to be designated as Invariant. The Document may contain zero Invariant Sections. If the Document does not identify any Invariant Sections then there are none.

The „Cover Texts" are certain short passages of text that are listed, as Front-Cover Texts or Back-Cover Texts, in the notice that says that the Document is released under this License. A Front-Cover Text may be at most 5 words, and a Back-Cover Text may be at most 25 words.

A „Transparent" copy of the Document means a machine-readable copy, represented in a format whose specification is available to the general public, that is suitable for revising the document straightforwardly with generic text editors or (for images composed of pixels) generic paint programs or (for drawings) some widely available drawing editor, and that is suitable for input to text formatters or for automatic translation to a variety of formats suitable for input to text formatters. A copy made in an otherwise Transparent file format whose markup, or absence of markup, has been arranged to thwart or discourage subsequent modification by readers is not Transparent. An image format is not Transparent if used for any substantial amount of text. A copy that is not „Transparent" is called „Opaque".

Examples of suitable formats for Transparent copies include plain ASCII without markup, Texinfo input format, LaTeX input format, SGML or XML using a publicly available DTD, and standard-conforming simple HTML, PostScript or PDF designed for human modification. Examples of transparent image formats include PNG, XCF and JPG. Opaque formats include proprietary formats that can be read and edited only by proprietary word processors, SGML or XML for which the DTD and/ or processing tools are not generally available, and the machine-generated HTML, PostScript or PDF produced by some word processors for output purposes only.

The „Title Page" means, for a printed book, the title page itself, plus such following pages as are needed to hold, legibly, the material this License requires to appear in the title page. For works in formats which do not have any title page as such, „Title Page" means the text near the most prominent appearance of the work's title, preceding the beginning of the body of the text.

A section „Entitled XYZ" means a named subunit of the Document whose title either is precisely XYZ or contains XYZ in parentheses following text that translates XYZ in another language. (Here XYZ stands for a specific section name mentioned below, such as „Acknowledgements", „Dedications", „Endorsements", or „History".) To „Preserve the Title" of such a section when you modify the Document means that it remains a section „Entitled XYZ" according to this definition.

The Document may include Warranty Disclaimers next to the notice which states that this License applies to the Document. These Warranty Disclaimers are considered to be included by reference in this License, but only as regards disclaiming warranties: any other implication that these Warranty Disclaimers may have is void and has no effect on the meaning of this License.

VERBATIM COPYING

You may copy and distribute the Document in any medium, either commercially or noncommercially, provided that this License, the copyright notices, and the license notice saying this License applies to the Document are reproduced in all copies, and that you add no other conditions whatsoever to those of this License. You may not use technical measures to obstruct or control the reading or further copying of the copies you make or distribute. However, you may accept compensation in exchange for copies. If you distribute a large enough number of copies you must also follow the conditions in section 3.

You may also lend copies, under the same conditions stated above, and you may publicly display copies.

COPYING IN QUANTITY

If you publish printed copies (or copies in media that commonly have printed covers) of the Document, numbering more than 100, and the Document's license notice requires Cover Texts, you must enclose the copies in covers that carry, clearly and legibly, all these Cover Texts: Front-Cover Texts on the front cover, and Back-Cover Texts on the back cover. Both covers must also clearly and legibly identify you as the publisher of these copies. The front cover must present the full title with all words of the title equally prominent and visible. You may add other material on the covers in addition. Copying with changes limited to the covers, as long as they preserve the title of the Document and satisfy these conditions, can be treated as verbatim copying in other respects.

If the required texts for either cover are too voluminous to fit legibly, you should put the first ones listed (as many as fit reasonably) on the actual cover, and continue the rest onto adjacent pages.

If you publish or distribute Opaque copies of the Document numbering more than 100, you must either include a machine-readable Transparent copy along with each Opaque copy, or state in or with each Opaque copy a computer-network location from which the general network-using public has access to download using public-standard network protocols a complete Transparent copy of the Document, free of added material. If you use the latter option, you must take reasonably prudent steps, when you begin distribution of Opaque copies in quantity, to ensure that this Transparent copy will remain thus accessible at the stated location until at least one year after the last time you distribute an Opaque copy (directly or through your agents or retailers) of that edition to the public. It is requested, but not required, that you contact the authors of the Document well before redistributing any large number of copies, to give them a chance to provide you with an updated version of the Document.

MODIFICATIONS

You may copy and distribute a Modified Version of the Document under the conditions of sections 2 and 3 above, provided that you release the Modified Version under precisely this License, with the Modified Version filling the role of the Document, thus licensing distribution and modification of the Modified Version to whoever possesses a copy of it. In addition, you must do these things in the Modified Version:

Use in the Title Page (and on the covers, if any) a title distinct from that of the Document, and from those of previous versions (which should, if there were any, be listed in the History section of the Document). You may use the same title as a previous version if the original publisher of that version gives permission.

List on the Title Page, as authors, one or more persons or entities responsible for authorship of the modifications in the Modified Version, together with at least five of the principal authors of the Document (all of its principal authors, if it has fewer than five), unless they release you from this requirement.

State on the Title page the name of the publisher of the Modified Version, as the publisher.

Preserve all the copyright notices of the Document.

Add an appropriate copyright notice for your modifications adjacent to the other copyright notices.

Include, immediately after the copyright notices, a license notice giving the public permission to use the Modified Version under the terms of this License, in the form shown in the Addendum below.

Preserve in that license notice the full lists of Invariant Sections and required Cover Texts given in the Document's license notice.

Include an unaltered copy of this License.

Preserve the section Entitled „History", Preserve its Title, and add to it an item stating at least the title, year, new authors, and publisher of the Modified Version as given on the Title Page. If there is no section Entitled „History" in the Document, create one stating the title, year, authors, and publisher of the Document as given on its Title Page, then add an item describing the Modified Version as stated in the previous sentence.

Preserve the network location, if any, given in the Document for public access to a Transparent copy of the Document, and likewise the network locations given in the Document for previous versions it was based on. These may be placed in the „History" section. You may omit a network location for a work that was published at least four years before the Document itself, or if the original publisher of the version it refers to gives permission.

For any section Entitled „Acknowledgements" or „Dedications", Preserve the Title of the section, and preserve in the section all the substance and tone of each of the contributor acknowledgements and/or dedications given therein.

- Preserve all the Invariant Sections of the Document, unaltered in their text and in their titles. Section numbers or the equivalent are not considered part of the section titles.
- Delete any section Entitled „Endorsements". Such a section may not be included in the Modified Version.
- Do not retitle any existing section to be Entitled „Endorsements" or to conflict in title with any Invariant Section.
- Preserve any Warranty Disclaimers.

If the Modified Version includes new front-matter sections or appendices that qualify as Secondary Sections and contain no material copied from the Document, you may at your option designate some or all of these sections as invariant. To do this, add their titles to the list of Invariant Sections in the Modified Version's license notice. These titles must be distinct from any other section titles.

You may add a section Entitled „Endorsements", provided it contains nothing but endorsements of your Modified Version by various parties— for example, statements of peer review or that the text has been approved by an organization as the authoritative definition of a standard.

You may add a passage of up to five words as a Front-Cover Text, and a passage of up to 25 words as a Back-Cover Text, to the end of the list of Cover Texts in the Modified Version. Only one passage of Front-Cover Text and one of Back-Cover Text may be added by (or through arrangements made by) any one entity. If the Document already includes a cover text for the same cover, previously added by you or by arrangement made by the same entity you are acting on behalf of, you may not add another; but you may replace the old one, on explicit permission from the previous publisher that added the old one.

The author(s) and publisher(s) of the Document do not by this License give permission to use their names for publicity for or to assert or imply endorsement of any Modified Version.

COMBINING DOCUMENTS

You may combine the Document with other documents released under this License, under the terms defined in section 4 above for modified versions, provided that you include in the combination all of the Invariant Sections of all of the original documents, unmodified, and list them all as Invariant Sections of your combined work in its license notice, and that you preserve all their Warranty Disclaimers.

The combined work need only contain one copy of this License, and multiple identical Invariant Sections may be replaced with a single copy. If there are multiple Invariant Sections with the same name but different contents, make the title of each such section unique by adding at the end of it, in parentheses, the name of the original author or publisher of that section if known, or else a unique number. Make the same adjustment to the section titles in the list of Invariant Sections in the license notice of the combined work.

In the combination, you must combine any sections Entitled „History" in the various original documents, forming one section Entitled „History"; likewise combine any sections Entitled „Acknowledgements", and any sections Entitled „Dedications". You must delete all sections Entitled „Endorsements".

COLLECTIONS OF DOCUMENTS

You may make a collection consisting of the Document and other documents released under this License, and replace the individual copies of this License in the various documents with a single copy that is included in the collection, provided that you follow the rules of this License for verbatim copying of each of the documents in all other respects.

You may extract a single document from such a collection, and distribute it individually under this License, provided you insert a copy of this License into the extracted document, and follow this License in all other respects regarding verbatim copying of that document.

AGGREGATION WITH INDEPENDENT WORKS

A compilation of the Document or its derivatives with other separate and independent documents or works, in or on a volume of a storage or distribution medium, is called an „aggregate" if the copyright resulting from the compilation is not used to limit the legal rights of the compilation's users beyond what the individual works permit. When the Document is included in an aggregate, this License does not apply to the other works in the aggregate which are not themselves derivative works of the Document.

If the Cover Text requirement of section 3 is applicable to these copies of the Document, then if the Document is less than one half of the entire aggregate, the Document's Cover Texts may be placed on covers that bracket the Document within the aggregate, or the electronic equivalent of covers if the Document is in electronic form. Otherwise they must appear on printed covers that bracket the whole aggregate.

TRANSLATION

Translation is considered a kind of modification, so you may distribute translations of the Document under the terms of section 4. Replacing Invariant Sections with translations requires special permission from their copyright holders, but you may include translations of some or all Invariant Sections in addition to the original versions of these Invariant Sections. You may include a translation of this License, and all the license notices in the Document, and any Warranty Disclaimers, provided that you also include the original English version of this License and the original versions of those notices and disclaimers. In case of a disagreement between the translation and the original version of this License or a notice or disclaimer, the original version will prevail.

If a section in the Document is Entitled „Acknowledgements", „Dedications", or „History", the requirement (section 4) to Preserve its Title (section 1) will typically require changing the actual title.

TERMINATION

You may not copy, modify, sublicense, or distribute the Document except as expressly provided for under this License. Any other attempt to copy, modify, sublicense or distribute the Document is void, and will automatically terminate your rights under this License. However, parties who have received copies, or rights, from you under this License will not have their licenses terminated so long as such parties remain in full compliance.

FUTURE REVISIONS OF THIS LICENSE

The Free Software Foundation may publish new, revised versions of the GNU Free Documentation License from time to time. Such new versions will be similar in spirit to the present version, but may differ in detail to address new problems or concerns. See http://www.gnu.org/copyleft/.

Each version of the License is given a distinguishing version number. If the Document specifies that a particular numbered version of this License „or any later version" applies to it, you have the option of following the terms and conditions either of that specified version or of any later version that has been published (not as a draft) by the Free Software Foundation. If the Document does not specify a version number of this License, you may choose any version ever published (not as a draft) by the Free Software Foundation.

ADDENDUM: How to use this License for your documents

To use this License in a document you have written, include a copy of the License in the document and put the following copyright and license notices just after the title page:

> Copyright (c) YEAR YOUR NAME. Permission is granted to copy, distribute and/or modify this document under the terms of the GNU Free Documentation License, Version 1.2 or any later version published by the Free Software Foundation; with no Invariant Sections, no Front-Cover Texts, and no Back-Cover Texts. A copy of the license is included in the section entitled „GNU Free Documentation License".

If you have Invariant Sections, Front-Cover Texts and Back-Cover Texts, replace the „with...Texts." line with this:

> with the Invariant Sections being LIST THEIR TITLES, with the Front-Cover Texts being LIST, and with the Back-Cover Texts being LIST.

If you have Invariant Sections without Cover Texts, or some other combination of the three, merge those two alternatives to suit the situation. If your document contains nontrivial examples of program code, we recommend releasing these examples in parallel under your choice of free software license, such as the GNU General Public License, to permit their use in free software.

Colophon

This work is licensed under the GNU Free Documentation License. It was originally written in LaTeX, then ported to DocBook. It is available in transparent copy in the DocBook/XML format. A build system and special instructions on processing are part of the transparent copy package, though building from the source is system dependent. The source can be built into either HTML or PDF format, and extension to other formats should be possible and is encouraged.

The original version of this document was written by Robert L. Read without renumeration and dedicated to the programmers of Hire.com.

Change Log

10/17/2008   Changed the title to „"Robert Read's How To Be A Programmer" - Feinhochburg editorial board
10/15/2008 Shortened the subtitle to "A Comprehensive Summary"
10/10/2008 Added an index - Elpidio Latorilla

10/08/2008 Removed the reference numbers [2 and [3 - E. Latorilla

10/06/2008 Corrected typo errors - Elpidio Latorilla

10/02/2008 Changed chapter format - Elpidio Latorilla

Index

Index

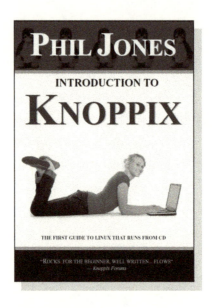